Hezekiah Butterworth

Zigzag Journeys in the Levant

Hezekiah Butterworth

**Zigzag Journeys in the Levant**

ISBN/EAN: 9783744753302

Printed in Europe, USA, Canada, Australia, Japan

Cover: Foto ©Andreas Hilbeck / pixelio.de

More available books at **www.hansebooks.com**

# The Zigzag Series.

### BY
### HEZEKIAH BUTTERWORTH.

ZIGZAG JOURNEYS IN EUROPE.
ZIGZAG JOURNEYS IN CLASSIC LANDS.
ZIGZAG JOURNEYS IN THE ORIENT.
ZIGZAG JOURNEYS IN THE OCCIDENT.
ZIGZAG JOURNEYS IN NORTHERN LANDS.
ZIGZAG JOURNEYS IN ACADIA.
ZIGZAG JOURNEYS IN THE LEVANT.
ZIGZAG JOURNEYS IN THE SUNNY SOUTH.
ZIGZAG JOURNEYS IN INDIA.
ZIGZAG JOURNEYS IN THE ANTIPODES.

**ESTES AND LAURIAT, Publishers,**
BOSTON, MASS.

SARDANAPALUS.

IN

# THE LEVANT,

## WITH A TALMUDIST STORY-TELLER.

*A SPRING TRIP OF THE ZIGZAG CLUB THROUGH EGYPT
AND THE HOLY LAND.*

BY

HEZEKIAH BUTTERWORTH,

AUTHOR OF "POEMS FOR CHRISTMAS, EASTER, AND NEW YEAR," "YOUNG FOLKS' HISTORY OF AMERICA,"
"ZIGZAG JOURNEYS IN EUROPE," ETC.

FULLY ILLUSTRATED.

BOSTON:
ESTES AND LAURIAT,
301-305 Washington Street.

T is one aim of this volume to amuse and entertain. But the writer has a deeper purpose in this book, and in all the books of this series. It is to interest young people in history and heroic records, and especially in the *present* political history of the countries to which the journeys are supposed to be made.

Young people should be made intelligent about the politics of other lands. The writer has endeavored to give, in this volume, as clear a view as possible of the present aspects of the Eastern questions, and of the governments of the countries of the Levant; so that when a young reader of the book shall see telegrams from the East in regard to political movements, he may better understand them, and be able to follow current history as it shall be recorded by the telegraph.

A like aim underlies the stories and narratives of all this series of books, — to lay the foundation for better reading, for a broader political intelligence.

The writer is indebted to Mrs. Andrews, of Hamilton, N. Y., for the descriptive parts of the two chapters on Greece.

H. B.

# CONTENTS.

| Chapter | | Page |
|---|---|---|
| I. | Old Ali Bedair | 15 |
| II. | Some Curious Stories | 31 |
| III. | Nights in London and a Night in Ancient Thebes | 51 |
| IV. | Cost of Journeys in the Levant | 67 |
| V. | To the Mediterranean | 84 |
| VI. | To the Pyramids | 100 |
| VII. | The Ruins of the Queen City of the World | 125 |
| VIII. | A Digression. — Egyptian Antiquities in Boston | 158 |
| IX. | History of England in Egypt | 197 |
| X. | The Joy of the Whole Earth | 211 |
| XI. | "Even unto Bethlehem" | 239 |
| XII. | The Sultan and Palestine | 261 |
| XIII. | Athens | 267 |
| XIV. | The New Greek Empire | 291 |

# ILLUSTRATIONS.

| | PAGE | | PAGE |
|---|---|---|---|
| Sardanapalus . . . . . . . . *Frontispiece.* | | An Egyptian Villa | 107 |
| A Ford of the River Jordan | 17 | Brick Pyramid of Faioum | 109 |
| Egyptian Garden and Temple | 21 | Donkey Boys | 111 |
| Travelling in the East | 25 | Pyramids and Sphinx | 115 |
| The Mode of Obeisance | 27 | Rameses | 117 |
| Arab and Ass | 29 | Medinet, Court of Rameses | 118 |
| A Merchant starting on a Journey in Palestine | 33 | Triumphal Car of Sesostris | 119 |
| | | Medinet, Temple-palace of Rameses | 123 |
| The Dog watching Abel's Body | 36 | Duck-shooting on the Nile | 127 |
| Camel in the Desert | 37 | Vultures in Egypt | 131 |
| Plain and Obelisk of Heliopolis | 39 | Falls of the Nile | 135 |
| A Family moving in the East | 41 | Coptic Maiden | 137 |
| View on the Road from Jerusalem to Jericho | 45 | Karnak, Hypostyle Hall | 139 |
| | | Karnak, Exterior Wall | 141 |
| Mount Ararat | 47 | Court of the Colossi | 143 |
| On the Upper Nile | 49 | The Dealer in Antiquities | 147 |
| Egyptian Curiosities | 53 | Cats | 151 |
| The Demavend | 57 | Snake-charming | 155 |
| Peasants reaping in the Field | 61 | Egyptian Ruin | 159 |
| Ruins of Thebes | 65 | Façade in Mexico | 169 |
| Winged Bull, Assyria | 69 | Egyptian-like Ruins in Mexico | 173 |
| Merchant and Camel | 73 | The Sacks of Wine leaking | 175 |
| Winged Bull from Nineveh | 76 | Leaving his Arm behind | 177 |
| Hanging Gardens of Babylon | 77 | The Mameluke's Leap | 183 |
| Palace of Nineveh | 80 | The Slave was borne away | 185 |
| Grand Hall of Assyrian Museum | 81 | Dervishes | 187 |
| Interior of a Palace, Seville | 87 | Defile in the Road from Palestine to Egypt | 190 |
| The Rock of Gibraltar | 91 | | |
| The Funeral Procession | 93 | An Egyptian Town | 191 |
| Hannibal swearing Eternal Hatred to the Romans | 95 | Scene on the Nile | 205 |
| | | Boats on the Nile | 209 |
| Hannibal on an Expedition | 97 | Hills and Walls of Jerusalem | 212 |
| Alexander the Great | 103 | Jerusalem | 213 |

|  | PAGE |  | PAGE |
|---|---|---|---|
| The Mosque of Omar | 216 | The Grand Range of Lebanon | 251 |
| Interior of the Mosque of Omar | 217 | Mount of Olives | 253 |
| The Jews' Place of Wailing | 220 | Grotto of the Nativity, Bethlehem | 256 |
| Jerusalem from the Mount of Olives | 221 | Vale and City of Nazareth | 257 |
| The Holy Sepulchre | 224 | The Suburbs of Athens | 269 |
| View in the Valley of the Jordan | 225 | Port of Piræus | 273 |
| Coming to see the Miracle | 229 | The Athenian Carnival | 277 |
| The Queen of Sheba | 232 | The Parthenon | 281 |
| The Queen of Sheba and Solomon | 235 | Travelling in Greece | 283 |
| The Pools of Solomon | 236 | Hermonthis | 285 |
| Bethlehem | 240 | An Arab Boy | 289 |
| Bethlehem | 241 | A Fountain in Greece | 294 |
| Ruth | 245 | Ruins of a Temple in Greece | 295 |
| The Castle of David, and Jaffa Gate | 250 |  |  |

# THE LEVANT

## CHAPTER I.

### OLD ALI BEDAIR.

### THE JEWISH INTERPRETER.

THE autumn of 188- Charlie Leland, one of the members of the Zigzag Club, was in London. He had gone there with his father, a Boston merchant, who had become a nervous sufferer by prolonged application to business. Physicians had recommended to Mr. Leland an immediate change of scene; and he had suddenly left for London, taking Charlie with him.

Charlie greatly loved his father's companionship. The friendship between fathers and sons is a pleasing feature of Boston life. It is not an uncommon thing for a Boston boy to choose his own father for his confidential companion and most intimate friend.

Mr. Leland and his son might often have been seen taking arm-in-arm walks into the beautiful suburbs of Boston, — over the Mill Dam road, or into the cool woods of the fenceless Roxbury Park, or making late summer excursions into that miniature Rocky Mountain region known as Middlesex Fells.

In London, the two were constantly together. In the mornings they visited the art galleries, and in the afternoons often went to Regent Park, or Hyde Park and Rotten Row, or, when the weather was warm, read the London journals on the hospitable benches of St. James's Park. Sometimes they went to Sydenham Palace, and often to suburban places made famous by history or poetry.

They often passed a part of the evening at the American Exchange, in reading the American journals, of which few reading-rooms in the United States have so large a supply.

One night, as they were sitting together here, an aged man entered the room in Oriental costume; and his benevolent face and somewhat peculiar habits attracted the attention of both father and son. The Oriental visitor — for such he seemed to be — took no notice of the papers that covered the tables and walls of the room, but went to one of the windows and gazed abstractedly into the gas-lighted air, and towards the luminous windows of Charing Cross Hotel.

The streets, like rivers, were pouring a vast population into the Strand, — people seeking various halls, churches, and places of amusement. The old man watched the gay forms as they passed ever on and on, coming out of the night and vanishing into the night. The street was filled with cabs and hansoms, crowded 'buses and elegant private vehicles. Near by the bells of St. Martin's were striking; but the happy hearts on the street were only made lighter by the musical notes that marked the passing of time.

The entrance to the Strand on an autumn evening is a tide of human life. The scene must have been strange to Oriental eyes; all the overflow of gayety, prosperity, and splendor. The old man's gaze seemed riveted on the kaleidoscope; a half-hour passed, the bell of St. Martin's struck again, but he did not move.

Mr. Leland, having finished his reading of the Boston papers received by the latest steamer, went to the window where the old

A FORD OF THE RIVER JORDAN.

man was standing, and looked for a time at the hundreds of vehicles passing by Charing Cross.

"A beautiful night," said Mr. Leland.

"Night," answered the old man, in pure English, — "night! There is no night here, — the people have banished the night of God, — no sky, no stars. Night visits the desert, night visits the sea; the people here never see the night. Come to Cairo and I will show you the night, and read to you the poetry of the night."

"You are from the East?"

"Yes, from the East; and you?"

"From America."

"America, — so far away, so far away. I have travelled with Americans. Good people, — Americans! I love Americans."

He touched his heart, and turned towards the door, saying, —

"So far away."

A few days after, while Mr. Leland and Charlie were visiting, it may be for the twentieth time, the Turner pictures in the National Gallery, the same old man appeared. He passed them without noticing them at first; but on slowly recrossing the room, he recognized Mr. Leland, and saluted him by a wave of the hand. He then bent his dark eyes on Charlie, and his face lighted up with such a smile of good will that the boy's face responded in sympathy. The old man waved his hand again, this time to Charlie; then moved on, saying, —

"So far away."

"What a benevolent face!" said Charlie to his father. "I wish I knew him. There is something about him that interests me, and that I like."

A week passed. One morning Mr. Leland and Charlie went into Westminster Abbey, and wandered almost alone among the chapels of dead heroes, benefactors, and kings.

They stopped before the Wesley tablets, and read the inscriptions.

"'God buries his servants, but his work goes on!'" said Mr. Leland, repeating meditatively what he had just been reading. "I did not expect to find a memorial of the Wesleys here. The founders of Methodism were excluded in their day from fellowship with the English church, and their names are now made to ornament the Abbey. Truly, 'they that turn many to righteousness —'"

"'Shall shine as the stars,'" said a voice, like an echo.

Mr. Leland turned. Near him stood the figure of the old Oriental, his face beaming with pleasure.

He waved his hand. "I am glad that thou lovest the poetry of the prophets," he said.

He waved his hand to Charlie, his face again lighting up with an amiable smile. There was a burst of organ music; and the old man turned slowly towards another part of the Abbey, saying, as before, —

"So far away."

Mr. Leland and Charlie sat down to listen to the organ.

"I have read many books," said Charlie, "about the kings who are buried here." Then referring to memorials like the Wesleys', he added: "I wish some one would write a book about the benefactors whose names are here, and who *crowned themselves* kings of men by the struggles of their own lives. I am more impressed by these memorials than by anything else I have seen. The tombs of the kings in comparison seem to me to be only stone, dust, and rubbish."

"Deeds are the true crown of life," said Mr. Leland.

"Let us go and look again at the Coronation Stone," said Charlie.

The stone was set into the frame of the throne chair. Mr. Leland and Charlie stood looking upon it with the doubt with which most Americans are accustomed to view legendary relics. A light, slow footstep was heard on the stone floor, and the sound betrayed the approach of the odd Oriental figure that they had met before.

The old man said to a custodian, —

EGYPTIAN GARDEN AND TEMPLE

"Jacob's?"

The doughty custodian bobbed his head.

A beautiful light came into the old man's face.

"Adam's?"

The doughty Englishman shook his head with an expression of disgust.

"Jacob's 'ead laid on that stone when he dreamed of the ladder of angels," said the custodian.

"That stone was twelve stones once," said the old man. "The twelve stones were the altar of Adam."

"*Adam!*" said the amazed custodian, having never before heard such a great antiquity attributed to the relic.

"Abel offered his sacrifice upon them," said the old man. "And," he added, "Abraham made his altar of them."

"Look 'ere! you are a Jew!" said the fat little Englishman. "My conscience is not quite easy when I tell people that that is the stone where Jacob saw the vision," he said to Mr. Leland; "and 'ere comes a man who says the stone is as old as *Adam*."

"The twelve stones became a single pillow when Jacob laid his head upon them," said the old man, reverently.

Charlie could see no evidences of such an assimilation, and even the custodian had never observed any latent marks of the alleged miraculous transformation.

"May I ask you who you are?" said the custodian to the old man.

"They call me the Talmudist, — Ali Bedair. I am an interpreter, and travel with parties in the East."

The old man moved slowly away, with a gentle sweep of his hand to Charlie, whose eyes followed him.

"A character," said the custodian to Mr. Leland. "London is full of characters, especially Jewry."

A service had commenced in the Abbey. The seats were partly filled with people with prayer-books. In one of the seats were four

American young ladies, returning to America from Italy by the way of London.

Mr. Leland and Charlie took a seat behind them.

The young ladies seemed devoutly given to their prayer-books, as strangers would be expected to be under the inspirations of the solemn Abbey. The music was almost celestial; the surpliced choir rose and disappeared, like a vision; the ancient liturgy was echoed from the tombs of scores of silent poets, and a hundred princes, and all the kings. The devotion of the young ladies to their books was absorbing. The service closed.

"There," said one of the ladies. "I have read all this book says, and now I am ready for the sights."

"I've read mine," said the second. "Mine is Baedeker's. What is yours?"

"Murray's," said the third.

"Mine is the 'London Guide Book,'" said the fourth.

"We haven't lost any time, have we?" said the first.

"No!" thankfully answered the other three.

"This is a queer world," said Mr. Leland.

"Let us go," said Charlie. "I am ashamed of our own people; but I wish I could meet that old Jew again. There is something I like about him,— he interests me, I cannot tell how or why. He seems like a poet, like a patriarch, like a wise man of an Arabian story. What is a *Talmudist?*"

Mr. Leland was unable to say. The meeting of a Talmudist in London was an unexpected episode, and one for which none of the guide-books had made any provision.

"Do you think that we shall see him again?" asked Charlie.

"I do not know."

"If we do, I am sure that we shall know him."

"Yes, quite sure," said Mr. Leland, with a smile. "I should be likely to know *him* anywhere."

TRAVELLING IN THE EAST.

The gray weeks of late November and early December passed. London grew cold and dark; and Mr. Leland decided to go South, and spend the January and February of the new year in a brighter and warmer atmosphere. Where? Nice was thought of; Majorca was discussed; Rome, Naples, Amalfi. Then the Levant presented its vision of grand antiquities. Mr. Leland preferred Nice; but Charlie was eager for a boat or tent journey in the lands of the rising sun, down the Nile to Thebes, or from Egypt over the track of the Israelites to Jerusalem, and thence to Damascus, the most ancient city in the world.

Days were passed in indecision. Charlie became accustomed to greet his father each morning with the question, —

"Is it the Levant?"

The lands of the Levant are properly those that lie upon and stretch away from the eastern shores of the Mediterranean, the lands of the sunrise; but these comprise territories so important and historic that the word *Levant* has come to be applied to the entire East.

Christmastide came. London became white and green; the air was full of bells, and the churches of music.

"Is it the Levant?" said Charlie to his father one day soon after Christmas.

"If I could secure good travelling companions, it would be the Levant. I learned," he added, "a curious matter yesterday from the card-writer in the Charing Cross Hotel. It will interest you. You remember the old Jew, — the Talmudist?"

"That we met in Westminster Abbey and at other places?"

THE MODE OF OBEISANCE.

"Yes. Well, it has been his business for years to accompany English travellers from Cairo to Jerusalem by the way of the Sinai Peninsula. I wish we could meet him again. He has a good reputation for character, amiability, and intelligence."

New Year's eve came. Early in the evening Mr. Leland and Charlie went to a service in the Methodist chapel at Bunhill Fields, where the pioneers of Methodism had preached; and they here visited John Wesley's house, which is close to the chapel.

Late in the evening they took a cab for London Bridge, and were left there to hear the bells of the city at midnight announce the New Year.

It was a glorious night. The weather had become mild, after some days of severe cold. The moon was mirrored in the Thames, the gray towers were illumined with a mystic light, and the streets overflowed with people.

At midnight all the bells of the city rang out over the great wilderness of homes, as Tennyson has voiced them in "In Memoriam." While all the air was thus throbbing with joyful music, a bent form slowly passed Mr. Leland, then paused.

"Beautiful," said the old man, — "beautiful; but sweeter to my ears would have been the bells upon the hem of the ephod, or even the tinkling of the camel's bell. Is it not beautiful?"

Mr. Leland and Charlie had again met the Jew; and the three walked in company, in the early morning of the New Year, towards Charing Cross and Trafalgar Square. When Mr. Leland parted from the old man he said to Charlie, —

"It is the Levant."

The next day Charlie cabled home: "*The Levant — Egypt — Palestine.*"

## CHAPTER II.

#### SOME CURIOUS STORIES

###### PATRIARCHAL LEGENDS FROM THE TALMUD.

LELAND and Charlie had taken rooms at the old Golden Cross Hotel, near Trafalgar Square. Close by was the Charing Cross Hotel, in itself a city of people from all civilized lands. Ali Bedair had apartments, not in Old Jewry, but here; and on parting from the Lelands at the foot of the Nelson Statue on New Year's morning, he graciously said, —

"I hope my friends from the West will do me the honor to call upon me. I shall be glad to tell you about the Eastern journey that you propose to make. I wish I might accompany you."

He added to Charlie, —

"If it be in your heart to visit an old man like me, I should be glad to welcome you. I once had a son. — My card."

The old man's invitation was accepted by Mr. Leland and Charlie for the next evening. In the mean time Mr. Leland made it his business to learn as much as possible about his new Oriental acquaintance.

Ali Bedair was well known among lovers of Eastern travel in London. All who had met him commended him.

"He is a mysterious old man of a most beautiful spirit," said one.

"He has the heart of a woman and the mind of a poet," said another.

"He is the loveliest old man that I ever knew in any land," said a lady of rank who had travelled with him.

"Ali Bedair is a story-teller," said a fourth. "He knows the Talmud by heart, and all the old legends and traditions of the East, whether Jewish or Mohammedan. Speak to him of any patriarch or prophet, and he will relate stories of him of which few Christian people have ever heard; untrue they may be, — fables, — but most beautifully true in the lessons of life and duty that they teach. It is worth making a journey to listen to the stories of Ali Bedair."

Mr. Leland and Charlie found the old Jew in a simple room, that contrasted strangely with the general brightness and sumptuousness of the hotel palace. He received his visitors most graciously. Turning up the gas-light, he said, —

"A single light answers as well for three men as for one, and for a hundred. Praise the Lord! My rooms are simple," he added. "But the place honors not the man, but the man the place. I would I were worthier."

An hour or more was spent in conversation about journeys from Egypt through Syria. Ali Bedair's information seemed inexhaustible, and his descriptions of places were most vivid and glowing. His attention for a time was wholly given to Mr. Leland. Then suddenly turning to Charlie, he said, —

"Pardon me, my son, I forget. 'Be affable to the young,' says a wise man. Shall you go with us, if we go?"

"It is my desire and ambition to go with you," said Charlie, warmly.

"I am glad to hear you say that, my son. I have tried as well as I could to answer your father's questions. Can I render a like service to you? I would be glad to do something for you."

He put his hand over his heart, and the simple words and gesture did not seem to be insincere. Charlie's affections were strongly drawn towards the gracious old man.

A MERCHANT STARTING ON A JOURNEY IN PALESTINE.

"There is one question I would like to ask," he said, "if it will not seem to you intrusive or personal. You said in the Abbey that you were a *Talmudist*. Father was not quite able to explain to me what a Talmudist is. Will you tell me?"

"That is an unexpected question," said the old man. "I would rather take another time to answer it. But the wise men say, 'Use thy beautiful vase to-day, for to-morrow it may break.'

"The Talmud is a commentary on the truths of the Scriptures, with illustrations of those truths in both history and fable. It is, or was, the oral law of our people, the collected wise thoughts of our nation for a thousand years. It comprises books of our history and traditions; it contains the sayings of our holiest and most learned men. It is a book of truths that men have learned by experience, and that time has proven to be true.

"The Talmud says to young men and to students like yourself: 'Add to your studies a trade, if you would keep your life free from sin.' This is wisdom and truth, but it does not claim direct spiritual inspiration as does a verse from the Sacred Scriptures. Do you see?

"The Talmud began with a record of the thoughts and experiences of wise men. It was preserved by the Schools of the Prophets, and each generation added to it new thoughts, proverbs, and illustrations. It was greatly used by the teachers in our synagogues. It was finally arranged in order and transcribed by Rabbi Judah and his sons, during the reign of the Roman Emperor Antoninus; and as such we find it to-day, though other rabbis have made additions to it. I will give you illustrations of it from time to time, should we travel together, which may God permit."

It was a lovely night. The statue of Nelson, which was seen from the high windows, seemed lifted into the sky from Trafalgar Square, and the clouds drifted white in the blue dome above it.

Ali Bedair sat by the window, and the night seemed to fill him with the spirit of his race and its ancient traditions. It was wonderful to listen to his quotations, his wit, and his fables. Charlie, impelled towards him by sympathy, drew his chair close to his.

"Tell me some of the ancient stories of Jewish people that are not found in the Scriptures," said Charlie.

"Shall they be true tales from the Talmud, or poetry?"

"Poetry."

"I do not mean verse, but allegory. Do you see?"

Story followed story, the old man selecting from Oriental traditions such as he thought that Charlie would most like to hear.

## ABEL'S SHEPHERD-DOG.

Cain was a tiller of the ground, and his brother Abel was a pastor of sheep.

The life of Abel was simple and pure, and was passed in the land of Adamah, where flowers from the seeds of Eden still bloomed.

He was attended in his pastoral duties by a shepherd dog, to whom he was always kind, and who became very much attached to his master.

THE DOG WATCHING ABEL'S BODY.

One day, Adam said to Cain and Abel: "My sons, ascend the mountain, and offer up sacrifices to the Ruler of the Earth and Heavens."

CAMEL IN THE DESERT.

Abel took from his flock his best sheep, and ascended to the mountain altar. Cain took a sheaf of corn, and one that was imperfect and useless.

The heavenly fire fell upon the offering of Abel, and the smoke mingled with the sky, but the sheaf of Cain remained untouched.

Jealousy, like an evil spirit, entered into the heart of Cain.

One day, Cain found Abel asleep on the mountain, with his dog by his side. Cain took a stone and dashed it against his head. He saw that he had killed his brother, and hurried away.

PLAIN AND OBELISK OF HELIOPOLIS.

The shepherd dog watched by the dead body of Abel as it lay still and cold upon the mountain side beneath the shadowy sun and the pitiful stars.

The body was discovered at last by Adam and Eve. The latter sat down beside it and wept. It was the first time that they had met Death in the world, and they knew not what to do.

A dark raven flew into a tree near them. He saw them weeping and pitied them. The raven had met Death before them; his mate had just died.

Then the raven said: "I will comfort Adam, and teach him how to hide the cause of his sorrow from the eye of day."

The raven dropped down from the tree in the sight of the sorrowful parents, and dug a hole in the earth. To this he presently brought the dead form of his mate, and covered it with earth.

Then said Adam to Eve: "We will do the same with Abel."

So they covered the form of Abel with earth, and blessed the dark raven who had taught them the lesson.

The raven was rewarded. From that day the raven has never asked Heaven for rain without bringing the world that blessing. The dog, as then, has ever proved the most faithful friend of man.

## PATRIARCHAL LEGENDS.

Shem, the son of Noah, became King of Salem. One day, one of the Patriarchs said to him,—

"What service did you and your father and brethren render to God while you were in the ark?"

"Charity," answered the king.

"How?" asked the Patriarch; "there was no one in the ark but yourselves."

"Even so; but we showed charity to the animals."

"How?"

"By kindness and attention. We sometimes did not sleep at night in order to make their condition comfortable."

The Patriarch expressed surprise.

"Once," continued the king, "when we had been delayed in feeding the beasts, a hungry lion sprung upon Noah, my father, and bit him."

"Then," said the Patriarch, "Noah was indeed a righteous man, if his charity extended to the dumb animals, and he bore with patience the injuries that their ignorance inflicted upon him. I will henceforth be more charitable to the poor, the wanderers, and the wayfarers."

A Patriarch searched for a grove and a fountain of water. When he found such a place, he built there a guest-house.

When a beggar or a traveller came to the guest-house hungry, he gave him meat and fruits; and when thirsty, he gave him water from the fountain.

"I thank thee," the guest would say to the Patriarch.

"Thank the Master. I am only a servant."

"Who is the Master?"

"The All-Merciful."

"How shall I worship him?"

"By returning thanks for all that he has done."

A FAMILY MOVING IN THE EAST.

## THE COURTSHIP OF JOSEPH.

The patriarch Joseph not only had a very tender heart, but he looked on the bright and hopeful side of all human concerns.

When he and his aged father met, they embraced and kissed each other.

"Now," said Jacob, "tell me, I pray thee, what evil thy brothers did unto thee when they betrayed and sold thee."

"Nay, my father," said Joseph, "let me tell thee only how good the Lord was to me."

The wife of Joseph was Asenath, a daughter of a Priest of the Sun. In her girlhood she was wonderfully beautiful. She dwelt in a tower ten stories high, surrounded by palm gardens, and she had everything that heart could desire.

She was an idol-worshipper. In her tower were idols of gold and silver to which she daily paid her devotions. But the beautiful Asenath had never been allowed to see a young man; so she ignorantly declared that she disliked the race of men, except only her father.

One day Joseph came to visit the old priest. He was seated in one of Pharaoh's chariots. The chariot was of solid gold, and was drawn by four white horses, with gilded reins.

Joseph was dressed in a tunic of gold, with a mantle of crimson. There was a fillet of gold about his temples, and he carried an olive branch in his hands.

When Asenath saw him she thought a sun god had come out of the brightness of the sky. She dared not look upon so much beauty, and she hastened to her chamber.

Now Joseph, before that he saw Asenath, had shunned the company of women.

Then said Joseph to the Priest of the Sun, —

"Where is the maiden who was here just now?"

"My lord, she has gone to her tower; for she is very modest, and has never seen the face of any man before to-day, save my own. I will send for her."

When Asenath again appeared the priest said, —

"My daughter, salute thy brother. He hateth women even as thou hatest men."

She approached Joseph to kiss his hand. But Joseph said, —

"I worship the living God, thy lips kiss dumb idols. Forbear, I pray thee."

Then Asenath began to weep, and the heart of Joseph was touched. He said to her,—

"Maiden, in eight days I will come to see thee again."

Asenath went to her tower, and cast her idols from the window. She dressed herself in black robes, and knelt down and prayed for the true light, which is brighter than the sun.

An angel saw her in Paradise. He pitied her, and gathered for her some honey from the roses whose odors filled all the air of that blissful region. He brought to her the honey, and when she had tasted it the true light came into her heart. She asked the angel to give a portion of the honey to her seven maidens, which he did, and they too received the inward light.

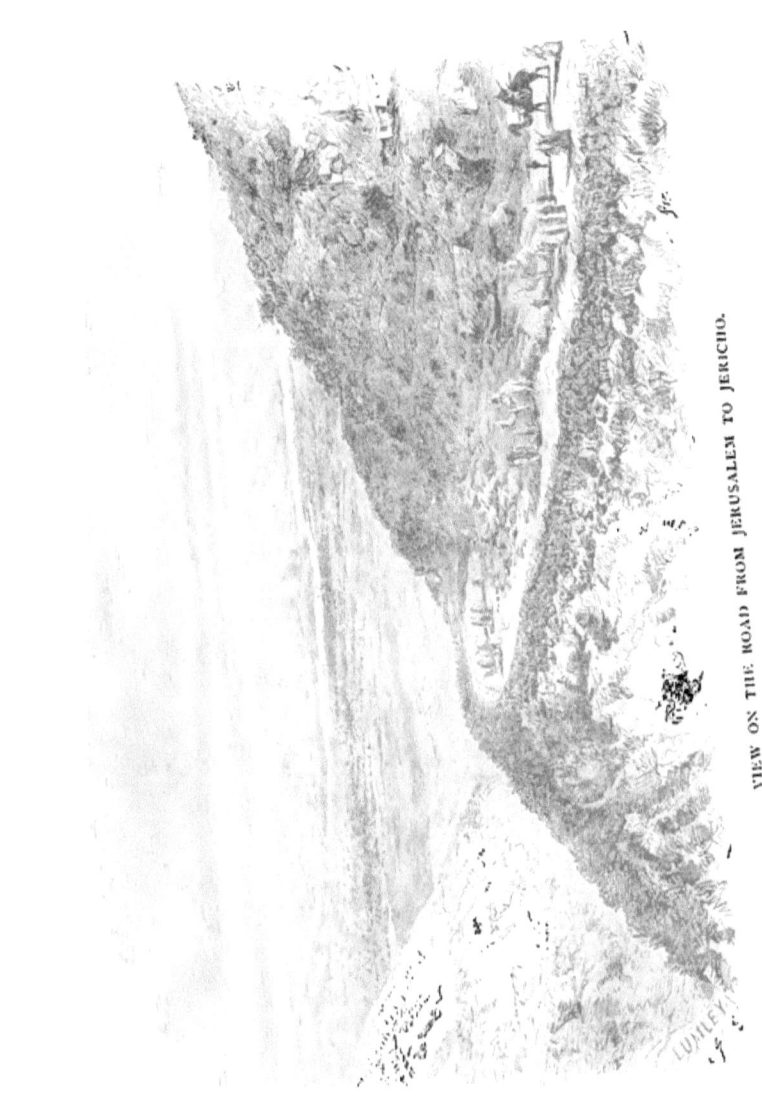

VIEW ON THE ROAD FROM JERUSALEM TO JERICHO.

"Rejoice," said the angel; "thy prayer is heard."
Instantly the aged Priest of the Sun opened the door, saying, —
"Joseph has come; prepare to meet him."
Joseph was told the story of the broken idols and the celestial honey, and he gladly received Asenath as his wife.

Charlie asked the Jew if he thought that these stories were true. He declined to say, but answered evasively, —
"All true poetry is the expression of truth."

MOUNT ARARAT.

The chimes of St. Martin told the hours, and the bell the quarters of the hour. As the bells announced the hour of eleven, the gracious old man laid his hand on Charlie's as it clasped the arm of his chair, and said, —
"Blessed is the son who has studied with his father, and happy is the father who himself instructeth his son."

There was something in his tone like a benediction, and Mr. Leland felt that it was time for him to rise and say good-night. Father and son crossed the street to the Golden Cross, with something of admiration for the lovely and helpful spirit so unexpectedly found in the Jew. Christians though they were, each felt that the visit had somehow proved helpful, and that the evening had been one of the most profitable in their lives.

ON THE UPPER NILE.

## CHAPTER III.

### NIGHTS IN LONDON AND A NIGHT IN ANCIENT THEBES.

A ZIGZAG JOURNEY PLANNED.—ALI BEDAIR'S POETICAL QUOTATIONS, AND HIS STORY OF THE LUCKY OLD MAN.

THE result of Mr. Leland's conference with Ali Bedair was that he would meet the latter at Alexandria, Egypt, early in March, and make a journey under his direction to Cairo, and down the Nile, and on returning, visit Palestine, arriving at Jerusalem in time to witness the celebration of Easter in April.

The doctors had advised Mr. Leland to spend much time on the sea; and he resolved to spend the interval of some five weeks at different ports of the Mediterranean, taking one of the trade steamers at Liverpool that plied between that port and the English ports in the Mediterranean, Malta and Cyprus, and that touched at Alexandria on its return.

Mr. Leland had found sight-seeing in London too exciting, and the voyage on the trade steamer would give him some weeks of comparative rest. He went to Liverpool to make the arrangements. He found excellent accommodations on a stanch vessel, where he and his son would be the only passengers. The steamer was restricted to no regular date, but would probably reach Alexandria before the middle of February, stopping some days at Cadiz, and for a short time at Gibraltar and Sicily as well as the English Mediterranean Isles. She would leave Liverpool about the middle of January.

Charlie Leland remained at the Golden Cross while his father was making these arrangements. The attachment that had suddenly sprung up between him and the aged Jew at Charing Cross grew; and the friendly feeling led to one of those companionships that sometimes arise between studious youth and ripe and scholarly age.

While Mr. Leland was absent, Wyllys Winn, an old member of the Zigzag Club, arrived in London, hoping to make an arrangement to take organ lessons with Best, a famous writer of music, an organ-teacher, and the organist of St. George's Hall, Liverpool. He immediately found Charlie Leland; and one of the first visits that he made in London was to be introduced by Charlie to his Oriental friend, Ali Bedair.

At this visit the gentle Talmudist made several quotations that the boys thought very striking and beautiful; and Charlie Leland made a note of them, as he wished to give thought to them when he should be alone.

He had asked the Jew about the precepts of the Talmud, when the latter at once made the quotation,—

"'He who refuses a precept to a pupil is guilty of a theft.'"

Old Ali Bedair was not to be thus guilty. He was never so happy as when he found ears for the proverbs that he had learned.

"You are students," he said, "I see,—students from the West. Listen, and I will give you some words that wiser and better men than many that live now, have handed down to those who seek instruction.

'Who is he who becomes wise?
He who is willing to learn something from all.
Who is he who becomes a conqueror?
He who learns to govern himself.

SACRED SYMBOLIC TREE.

ANCIENT LAMPS IN BRITISH MUSEUM.

IMPRESSIONS OF THE SIGNETS OF ANCIENT KINGS.

ANCIENT KNIVES.
From originals in the British Museum.

KING ON HIS THRONE.

EGYPTIAN CURIOSITIES.

> "Who is he who gains true riches?
> He who becomes content with his lot.
> Who is he who deserves the honor of men?
> It is he who himself honors men.'"

More poetic was the following: —

> "The iron breaks the stone,
> The fire melts the iron,
> The water extinguishes the fire,
> The wind dispels the cloud of water,
> A man withstands the wind,
> Fear overcomes the man,
> The wine-cup banishes fear,
> Sleep is more mighty than wine,
> Death is the master of Sleep,
> But Love is stronger than Death."

Very impressive was the following thought: —

> "Canst thou escape sin?
>     Where?
> Think whence thou comest,
> Think whither thou goest,
> Think before Whom thou shalt appear.
> Canst thou escape sin?
>     Where?"

And as full of wisdom, this: —

> "He who possesses a knowledge of God,
> And he who possesses a knowledge of men,
> Will see the consequences of sin;
> He will not take it upon his soul."

Again: —

> "The best preacher is the heart,
> The best teacher is experience (time);
> The best book is mankind,
> And the best friend is God."

Very simple and beautiful were the old man's views of life and its duties.

"Yesterday," he said, "is the past. I am living in the future. To-morrow — who has seen it? let me do my best now."

"Let me tell you, boys," he said, "about tent life in the East." Then followed a glowing and romantic description. Suddenly he paused and said, —

"My life is a tent. I am a pilgrim from afar to Jerusalem. Pray that my tent may fall at last before the Beautiful Gate of the Temple."

He related some poetic tales of Eastern fiction; among them the following about —

### THE LUCKY OLD MAN.

An Emperor was once passing through the streets of Tiberias when he noticed a very old man planting a fig-tree.

"Why do you plant trees?" asked the Emperor. "If thou hadst done such work in thy youth, thou wouldst be gathering figs to-day, instead of planting fig-trees. Thou canst not hope to eat the fruit of this tree."

"In my youth I labored for my own good," answered the old man; "in my old age I labor for the good of others. In my youth I gathered figs from trees that others had planted; other youth may eat of the trees that I plant. I must work in the sunset as at the sunrise, for the whole day is God's."

"How old art thou?" asked the Emperor.

"A hundred years."

"Do you expect to eat fruit from this tree?"

"If not, I will leave it to my son, as my father left orchards to me. That thought gives me pleasure. We live in future years already, in good intentions and dreams."

"Happy old man!" said the Emperor. "If thou dost live to gather figs from this tree, come and visit me at my palace, and I will reward thy labor."

Years passed. The old man lived, and the fig-tree grew. At last the tree filled with blossoms, then with figs. The old man gathered a basket of young figs, and taking his staff went to visit the Emperor.

"Well," asked the Emperor, "what is thy desire?"

"I am the old man whom, some years ago, you found planting a fig-tree. I was then a hundred years old. You told me then that if I ever lived to eat fruit from the tree to visit you, and therefore I am here. I have come to present you a basket of the figs."

THE DEMAVEND.

The Emperor gave the basket to one of his body-guard, and told him to take out of it the figs and to replace every fig by a gold coin.

The basket was returned to the old man. He looked into it, and was very happy; and he joyfully returned to his friends.

"Why didst thou so honor the old Jew?" asked one of the royal household of the Emperor.

"Because God had so honored him. God honors men first, the world afterwards."

Now there lived near the old man an old woman who was very envious and avaricious. When she heard of her neighbor's good fortune, she said to her husband, —

"Let us send a gift to the Emperor."

"What shall it be?"

"Cocoanuts," said the old wife.

"No, figs."

The old wife filled a large basket with figs, saying, —

"The more figs, the more coin. Now go, and you will return rich, like the Jew."

The old man came to the palace.

"Who are you?" demanded the guard.

"I have brought a present of figs for the Emperor."

"And what is your reason?"

"That he may replace them with coins."

The guard told the Emperor, who answered, —

"Take from him the figs, and pelt him with them; then order him to be gone. What has he done that I should honor him?"

The guard did so, accordingly; and the old man went home sorrowfully, and told his wife his reception and humiliation.

"But," he added, "I was lucky, after all."

"Lucky — how?"

"Suppose I had carried the cocoanuts?"

One evening, as Ali Bedair was walking along the Thames Embankment, with Mr. Leland and Charlie, he stopped on the stone balcony that looks out upon the bridges, where stands the Egyptian Obelisk. It is near the Charing Cross Station, where the night is never silent, and where the clocks of London are heard at short intervals, reminding the loiterer of the swiftness of passing time.

"This shaft of granite and gold," said the old interpreter, "looked down upon Egypt in the most splendid epoch of her history. Around us are some of the finest structures in the world, — St. Paul's, Westminster Abbey, the Parliament Houses, the Government Offices, Whitehall, and Trafalgar Square with its monument. This is London at night. Did you ever fancy Memphis at night, or ancient Thebes at night? Was the scene like this? Suppose this monument could speak, and reveal the scenes that have passed under its shadow!"

The three sat down on one of the public seats on the embankment near the monument, and the old man related to Charlie the following story: —

## A NIGHT AT ANCIENT THEBES.

It was night at ancient Thebes. The reflection of countless stars seemed like jewels sinking into the Nile. The moon, full orbed, like a sun of night, viewed her beauty in the calm waters.

Along the banks of the river palms rose like shadows. The air was fragrant with the odors of the lotus; the banks were paved with lilies; the margin of the waters was white with callas.

The city was silent. The pylons of temples with their hundred gates darkened the air. On one side of the valley rose the walls of the Libyan Mountains, a line of purple in the crystal air. On the other side were the mountains of Arabia, mysterious and dark, — a vast shadow-land.

The city, with its hill-climbing temples and its mountain tombs, covered an area of fifty miles. It was a city alike of the living and of the dead. Its history was lost in the traditions of mysterious epochs when gods governed the earth. Here slumbered the dead of four thousand years.

Silence! The palaces and temples were as still as the tombs in the hills. There had been a long festival; barges with silken banners had brocaded the Nile, and the down-going of the sun had been followed by the blaze of countless torches.

The Queen of Rome had come to visit the city of Menes. She had heard of the colossal sun-god called the Memnon; how it saluted the rising sun with chords from its lips of stone, whose music filled the air. Disregarded and

PEASANTS REAPING IN THE FIELD.

neglected by Hadrian, whose vices unfitted him for a true husband, the unhappy queen desired to hear the voice of a god ; for the gods of Rome had long ago ceased to speak.

The sleeping city was in itself a world. St. Paul's in London, in comparison to the temple palace of Sesostris, would be but a chapel ; the largest cathedral of the world to-day might have found room in those royal halls. The city of London to this wilderness of palaces and tombs would be indeed small. Buckingham Palace would then and there have been but a shed ; the Parliament Houses but light and unsubstantial structures.

The gates of the mighty temples were closed. From pylon to pylon vast avenues of sphinxes lifted their mysterious heads. There were hieroglyphics everywhere ; everywhere were the records of glory ; everywhere ruins.

On the side of the Libyan hills stood the Necropolis, where the priests of Osiris were interred. Kings slumbered there, whose names were already lost in the twilight of antiquity. Queens slept here, whose fame filled the world, but who now had not so much as a name. The kings had been conquerors ; now they were gods. The ancient kingdom, bounded on two sides by sky-clouding mountains, once stretched from the Cataracts to Mount Sinai.

Everything was colossal. Here histories were written in eternal stone. A single palace hall, with its cornices of beaten gold, was three hundred and twenty-nine feet long ; and this was followed by another of nearly equal length. Yet the ancient splendor of the city was gone ; Thebes even now was a ruin.

It was moonlight, — not the far-away, dim moon of the West, but an argent splendor, as though the Queen of Night had come down into the liquid regions of the air, and there floated on her throne.

And the moon that shone on Thebes and the Plain, shone on twenty thousand Egyptian cities, or their ruins.

Night wore on.

There were sweet sounds on the Nile, — bird-notes, the call of animals. The Day-spring had smiled already in the face of the Sphinx at Memphis. There was a stir in the streets. The Aurora was throwing her lances against the darkness of the east. The contest had begun between light and darkness.

A sea of fire seemed to flood the east. Millions of people filled the streets, and surrounded the hill-side temple of Memnon.

Would the statue speak to the Queen of Rome, as it had spoken to the dead queens in the Necropolis ?

Memnon had sung to the dawn before Rome was mighty, — when Egypt was the world, when captive nations built her monuments, and captive princes drew the chariots of the Pharaohs. Rome had humbled Egypt. Would the Son of Eos speak to the Roman Queen, now that the grandeur of Thebes was passed?

The Memnonium faced the rising sun. Its propylæon towered majestic in the air, for a distance so great that the temple itself seemed a city. The Circus still lifted its shadowy circle in the dusky and dewy air, out of each of whose hundred portals two hundred chariots once rolled to battle, or so might have rolled.

We have said that the city was a ruin. Thebes was believed to have been the oldest city on earth. It was old ere Rome was begun. When Memphis arose, Thebes began to decline. But though her ancient populations were diminished, her shadowy ruins still filled the plain and the hills. She was tottering to her final fall.

Morning upon the Nile is Paradise. The air is crystal in clearness, and the light falls upon the wings of countless birds, who drift on the perfumes with throats full of song.

Before the temple of Amenopis III., at the head of an army of decaying sphinxes, stood the statue of the vocal Memnon, that saluted Aurora with music. Cambyses had left the marks of his madness upon it, but the Memnon still uplifted its voice to the dawn.

The queen and her Roman nobles came out of the palace, and stood on an elevation whence they beheld both the east and the god.

The sky was now pale gold.

Slowly the rim of the sun began to appear. All Nature seemed to rejoice. The rays gilded the tops of the mountains; then they crowned the waiting propylæons of the city, and the ancient temple of Memnon.

They began to fall upon the head of the statue.

Hark! Do gods of stone indeed speak? Do they play upon harps?

There falls on the air a beautiful note. Now another. Seven.

Sabina listened in awe. The sun was now above the horizon.

"It was like a harp-note and not a voice," said a Roman noble.

"It is the harp of Egypt," said another.

"It is the harp of Egypt, indeed," said an Egyptian noble. "But did ye not hear? the harp-strings of Egypt seem breaking."

The harp of Memnon is broken! the voice of the god is still. On his broken throne and column may still be found inscribed these words: —

"I, Publius Balbinus, have heard the voice of the divine Memnon. I came in company with the Empress Sabina, at the first hour of the sun's course, the 15th year of the reign of Hadrian, the 25th of the month of November."

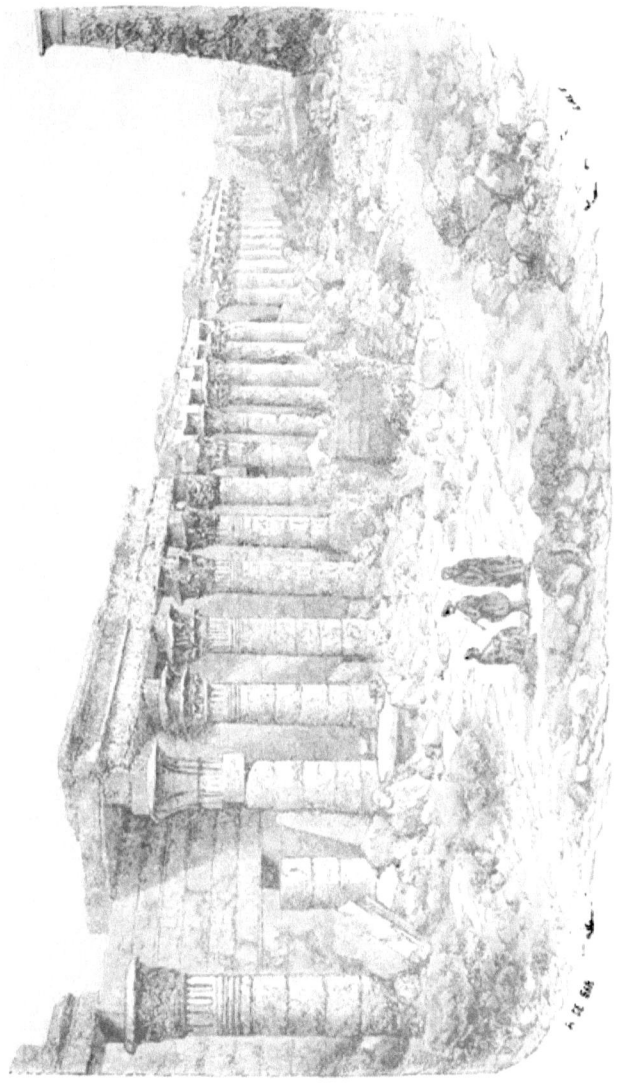

RUINS OF THEBES.

## CHAPTER IV.

#### COST OF JOURNEYS IN THE LEVANT.

##### STORY OF SEMIRAMIS AND SARDANAPALUS.

IT HAD been the intention of Mr. Leland to spend six months in travel, and to choose routes according to his own moods and inclinations. He was a man of ample means and generous impulses, and after twenty years' devotion to business, he wished that his six months' rest should be as free from care as possible.

One day, he and Charlie stepped over from the Golden Cross to the American Exchange, to see if there were any letters waiting for them, as several steamers had just arrived. Each had a liberal mail, and they sat down amid the piles of papers at the Exchange to read them.

"Father," said Charlie at length, "could a boy visit Egypt and Palestine for five hundred dollars?"

"From America? I think so. If he were to take second-class saloon fares on the steamer, and travel second class in Europe. He certainly could visit Alexandria, Cairo, Jerusalem, Bethlehem, and the Jordan for that sum. Why do you ask?"

"I have here a letter from Charlie Noble. He says that he writes in behalf of some of the schoolboys at Yule. How strange! He writes: 'Can we meet you at some Mediterranean port? Would your father be willing that we should accompany him to Cairo and Jerusalem?' What shall I answer?"

Charlie took up some stamped sheets from one of the writing-tables, and Mr. Leland began to gather around him the circulars of Cook, Gaze, and other travelling agents, and of the principal lines of steamers and railways.

"Say to Charlie Noble from me, 'Yes' and 'Come.'"

Charlie wrote, not quite knowing for whose benefit: "Father tells me to write 'Yes,' and 'Come.'"

"What shall I write next?"

"Say, 'Meet us at Gibraltar, Genoa, Venice, or Malta.'"

"Well."

"Say, 'The fare to London from New York on the National line, and from London to New York, round-trip ticket, would be $100, first class. By taking this route you would save connecting trips between Liverpool and London, and London and Liverpool, and from ten to fourteen dollars in money.'"

"Yes."

"Tell them, then,— whoever *them* may mean,— to take second-class railway tickets, Cook's or Gaze's, for Venice or Genoa, at a cost of about thirty dollars. The lowest price from London to Alexandria, Egypt, by these routes is about seventy dollars. The fare from London to Alexandria, by way of Paris, Turin, Genoa, and Rabattino steamer, on the Mediterranean, is $67.85. The cost of a Cook's ticket to Jerusalem from London, by way of Paris, Venice, and Austrian Lloyd's steamer, to Alexandria and Jaffa, is $93.45, second class."

"Less than one hundred dollars," said Charlie. "So one might go to Egypt and Palestine, or Alexandria and Jerusalem, from New York and return, for three hundred dollars?"

WINGED BULL, ASSYRIA.

"Three hundred dollars' fare. But that would hardly be a fair statement of the case."

"Could one make the trip for *less* than that?"

"One might take an intermediate passage on one of the Allan line of steamers from Quebec or Portland (winter), at forty dollars, and travel in Europe *third* class. I would not advise it, certainly not for a boy. The education of the company he might meet would not be likely to be always good.

"The Rabattino line of steamers, called also the Italian line, offer a fine trip for winter. These steamers sail from New York, and make a course so far south that ice, fog, and gales are generally avoided. They pass close to the Bermudas and the Azores, and are seldom more than three days distant from land. Let me enclose their present routes and rates: —

FROM NEW YORK.

|  | First Cabin. | Forward Saloon. |  | First Cabin. | Forward Saloon. |
|---|---|---|---|---|---|
| To Gibraltar | $90 | $60 | To Malta | $145 | $100 |
| " Marseilles | 110 | 70 | " Athens (Piræus) | 165 | 118 |
| " Genoa | 120 | 78 | " Smyrna, Salonica, Darda- | | |
| " Leghorn | 123 | 80 | nelles | 175 | 130 |
| " Naples | 130 | 88 | " Constantinople, Alexandria | 185 | 132 |
| " Messina, Palermo, Catania | 140 | 95 | " Odessa | 210 | 136 |

TO NEW YORK.

|  | First Cabin. | Second Cabin. |  | First Cabin. | Second Cabin. |
|---|---|---|---|---|---|
| From Odessa | $172 | $120 | From Genoa, Leghorn | $110 | $80 |
| " Constantinople | 154 | 110 | " Marseilles, Brindisi, | | |
| " Smyrna, Salonica, Dar- | | | Corfu, Malta | 110 | 80 |
| danelles | 146 | 106 | " Catania, Messina | 100 | 75 |
| " Alexandria | 138 | 102 | " Palermo, Naples | 100 | 75 |
| " Athens (Piræus) | 132 | 96 | Gibraltar | 85 | |
| Trieste, Venice, Ancona | 132 | 96 |  |  | |

"One might go to the Mediterranean in one of the steamers of this line, and return in one of the summer steamers of the Allan line to Quebec, through the grand river scenery of the St. Lawrence, by way of the Strait of Belle Isle. The Allan line of steamers in summer are usually only about four days on the open ocean out of sight of land, and sickness in any severe form is scarcely known during these trips. They are three days on the St. Lawrence, where the river scenery is among the grandest and most picturesque in America. The officers on these steamers are men of high character. I would recommend young people to travel as much as possible either by the *best* lines from New York and Boston, or the Allan line."

"Have the best lines from New York low rates of fares?"

"Some of the finest steamers have second-cabin fares. For example, look at these rates: —

ANCHOR LINE. *New York to Glasgow (calling at Moville).*
Saloon Fares, $60, $75, and $80.   Second Cabin Fares, $30.
Return Tickets, $110, $130, and $140.   Return Tickets, $60.

CUNARD LINE. *New York to Liverpool (calling at Queenstown).*
Saloon Fares, $60, $80, $100, and $125.   Return Tickets, $120, $144, $180, and $220.

GUION LINE. *New York to Liverpool (calling at Queenstown).*
Saloon Fares, $60, $80, and $100.   Second Cabin, $35.
Return Tickets, $120, $144, and $180.   Return Tickets, $70.

"One may sometimes take passage on fruit steamers direct to Sicily at a very low rate of fare."

"What shall I say about the cost of travel in the Levant?"

"The fare from Alexandria to Cairo by rail is only about five dollars."

"And then?"

"*Then?* — well, if the boys come, they shall be my guests for a boat journey up the Nile. '*Then?*' — they will be at Cairo in sight of the Pyramids."

"What will be the hotel rates?"

"On the Continent, $2.50 per day; in the Levant, $3.50. I will myself meet the expenses of our friends for the boat journey on the Nile. Say that we will be at Gibraltar on February 12; at Marseilles, Feb. 22; at Genoa, a few days later; and early in March at Alexan-

MERCHANT AND CAMEL.

dria. Tell them to take the National line to London, and meet us at Genoa."

"What is the usual cost of journeys to the Levant?"

"About a thousand dollars."

"Will it cost us each as much as that?"

"Unless your young friends should compel us to make short trips and use unexpected economy. Life on the Nile and journeys in Palestine are expensive. But Alexandria, Cairo, the Pyramids, Jerusalem, Bethlehem, and the Jordan may be visited by a tourist from America for five hundred dollars."

Mr. Leland did not trust to Charlie's letter to express his good-will towards any pupils of the school who might wish to make with him an Eastern journey. He sent a cable despatch to the teacher. He saw that a new arrangement as to the route would have to be made in order to meet the limited time and means at the disposal of the newcomers; but this he was willing to do.

In the mean time, as a preparation for the journey in the Levant, Mr. Leland and Charlie read Herodotus and Diodorus and other ancient books. Among the stories that proved very interesting to Charlie was that of —

## SEMIRAMIS AND SARDANAPALUS,

### THE FIRST QUEEN AND THE LAST KING OF NINEVEH.

In very ancient times there dwelt at Ascalon, in Syria, a very beautiful woman who was reputed to be a goddess. She became enamoured of a fair Syrian youth, and received him as her husband. A daughter was born, Semiramis.

But the mother became ashamed of her affection for the young Syrian, and seems to have desired again the reputation of a goddess rather than that of a frail human being; so she murdered her husband, and left her infant daughter in a secluded place to die.

WINGED BULL FROM NINEVEH.

Syria was full of doves. When these dwellers among the rocks came drifting down on their white wings into the solitude where the infant had been left to die, they pitied the helpless outcast, and, instructed by some good spirit, they fed it. They continued to feed it daily. So the infant Semiramis was nursed by the doves of Syria.

A Syrian shepherd at last discovered the infant, and brought her to the royal shepherd, whose name was Simmas. He took her into his household, and named her Semiramis.

Thus she grew up. She became famous, as she ripened into womanhood, for her beauty. She won the heart of Omnes, one of the king's friends and

HANGING GARDENS OF BABYLON.

generals, and he married her. She followed him to the army, and at the siege of Bactra she planned an assault that carried the citadel. She led the assault in person, and mounted the walls in triumph.

She was a heroine now, and regarded as one of the bravest and most beautiful women in the world. Ninus, the Assyrian king, admired her bravery and her beauty, and desired to make her his queen. She married him ; and Omnes, her former husband, was so deeply wounded by her desertion of him that he took his own life.

She was queen now, and her fame became so great as to shadow the glory of Ninus. One day, according to the ancient story, she came to the king with a request.

"O king, I have a favor to ask of thee."

"Thou hast but to ask it, and it shall be thine. What wouldst thou, Semiramis ? "

"I would be Queen of Asia for five days."

The request was granted. No sooner had she assumed the royal power than she cast the king into prison, and proclaimed herself the sovereign of all his empire. The beautiful Semiramis, like her mother, seems to have been a very dangerous wife to have.

If the last tradition be true, she still seems to have honored Ninus after his death ; for she erected a tomb to his memory nine stadia high, which was regarded as one of the wonders of the East.

Semiramis was a warrior. She was one of those ancient monarchs who conquered the world. Rameses II. (Sesostris) was but an imitator of the Assyrian queen. She not only subdued nearly all Asia, but conquered Egypt and Ethiopia. Her only failure was in India ; her invasions with this exception were triumphal marches.

She founded Babylon, constructed the hanging gardens of Media, built numerous cities, and erected some of the most extraordinary works of the East.

She reigned forty-two years.

Her death was like her infancy. The doves nursed her in the shepherd's country ; and her spirit, as it departed, took the form of a dove, and so mounted to the sky and the abodes of the immortal gods. So says mythology ; but in the light of to-day the dove would seem to be a very inappropriate emblem of the false heart and ambitious life of Semiramis.

According to Ctesias, the Assyrian empire of Nineveh lasted thirteen hundred and six years. It was founded by Ninus and Semiramis, and was reigned over by thirty effeminate kings, who succeeded one another in the relation of father and son in uninterrupted order, — a most marvellous record of history, could it be accepted as strictly true. By "effeminate" is meant kings without martial spirit, — devotees to pleasure rather than to ambition, to the arts of peace rather than to the arts of war. None of these kings, except the last, seems to have inherited the heroic spirit of Semiramis.

PALACE AT NINEVEH.

GRAND HALL OF ASSYRIAN MUSEUM.

indignant at the condition of the court and the empire. The Satrap of Media resolved to throw off his allegiance to such a weak and characterless monarch. He raised an army, and, supported by the Chaldean priesthood, advanced against Sardanapalus in Nineveh.

A change came over the monarch. The spirit of Semiramis seems to have been fettered within him, and by a tremendous struggle he broke the silken bonds. He rose superior to his weak and profitless habits and the inherited traits of his ancestors, and appeared before his army as a leader and warrior. He defeated his enemies in two great battles, but was finally besieged in Nineveh.

After a heroic struggle he saw that his hour had come and that Nineveh must fall. He ordered a funeral pile to be made, and he placed upon it the royal insignia and the treasures of his empire. He gathered around him his wives, generals, and friends. He then ordered the palace to be set on fire.

From a high place in the palace he saw the flames mounting around him. He saw the monuments of thousands of years changing into smoke, and the smoke clouding the air above him. He offered a libation to the gods from his golden wine-cup, dashed the cup to the earth, and with his favorite wife threw himself upon the pyre. Thus ended the Assyrian monarchy of Ninus.

## CHAPTER V.

### TO THE MEDITERRANEAN.

#### STORY OF DON JUAN. — HANNIBAL.

MR. LELAND invited Wyllys Winn to meet him in Alexandria early in March, and to make with the company the journey to the ruins of Thebes.

"I would like to do so," said Wyllys. "I had already thought of visiting the American School of Classical Studies at Athens during the year. Frank Gray, one of the old members of the Zigzag Club, is there, and he has invited me to visit him. But I must first hear from America, as my father pays my bills abroad. I do not dare to speak confidently," he added. "To visit the ruins of Thebes has been a dream for years. To visit them with you and Charlie and good old Ali Bedair would be to me the most delightful thing I can imagine. The experiences of which we dream in boyhood come true in later years. Thebes — I can shut my eyes and see it — there came to me an impression that I would one day behold its ruins, when I was studying ancient history at Yule."

"I know Professor Goodwin of Cambridge, Mass., who is now the director of the American School at Athens," said Mr. Leland.

"And I know Frank Gray," said Charlie. "I am going to write to him, and tell him about our plans for the Nile journey."

Late in January, Mr. Leland and Charlie left London for Liverpool, expecting to meet Ali Bedair at Alexandria early in March, and hoping that Wyllys Winn would join them there at the same time.

Liverpool is a city of ships. Her docks are five or more miles long. The city of ships on the sea is almost as large as the city of houses on the land.

It is a city of strangers. One may wander along the quays for hours amid crowds of men and heaps of merchandise, and nowhere in the world feel more utterly alone.

It is an event to stand near Victoria's Tower, and watch the rising tide of the Mersey, and the ships that wait outside of the harbor for the rising tide, in order to cross the Harbor Bar and come safely into port. The flags of all nations unite in the long commercial procession of peace, and a hundred anchors drop in the crimson twilight of the morning and evening under the gray walls of the salt-sea town.

"There is nothing to see at Liverpool," is a common expression. There is everything to see; in Liverpool one may see the world.

Mr. Leland and Charlie left Liverpool for Cadiz, going out of the winter gloom of the rugged English coast into the mild atmosphere and winds of the South. The steamer was booked to stop several days at Cadiz, and it was the intention of Mr. Leland to visit Seville while the ship should be detained at this port.

The winter voyage was somewhat tiresome. Charlie employed his time in reading ancient history, in writing letters to his friends in Boston and to Frank Gray at Athens.

Mr. Leland took with him a good supply of books which he wished Charlie to read during the long and broken voyage. Among them were Kitto's History of Palestine, Kitto's Cyclopædia, Smith's Classical

Dictionary, Layard's Works, Benoni, Gage's Palestine, Historical and Descriptive, Reland's Palestina, Arnold's Palestina, Boat-Life in Egypt, Herodotus, Diodorus, Abbott's History of Napoleon Bonaparte, Keith's Works, Homer, Virgil, Byron's Sardanapalus, Life of Alexander the Great, Lands of the Saracens, and a part of Abbott's Juvenile Histories.

At Cadiz our tourists were already in one of the ancient provinces of the Levant.

Cadiz was founded before Rome. In the times of the Spanish explorers it became a very important city, and gathered the riches of the Americas; when Spain lost her possessions in the Western World, it declined.

Steamships and railways again change the fortunes of Cadiz. A thousand ships now enter her harbor yearly. She strongly feels the impulses of that far Western World that her mariners discovered.

Seville — Sevilla, the ancient Hispalis — is situated on the left bank of the Guadalquivir, about one hundred miles from Cadiz. The traveller on a steamer that touches for a few days at Cadiz can easily visit Seville, by boat or rail.

The Moors built Sevilla from the ruins of Hispalis, and the Moorish walls and the outlines of the old city of Oriental splendors remain. The traveller here finds himself at once in an atmosphere of romance. The city is in the form of a circle. It is surrounded by walls that once contained one hundred and sixty-six towers, but now contain about sixty, and that once were pierced with fifteen or more historic gates. The old Moorish houses still blaze in the eye of the noontide sun, and seem to be beyond the reach of decay.

The city contains one hundred squares. We have spoken in another volume of its cathedral. Its palace rivalled the Alhambra. The Hall of the Ambassadors of this palace is one of the marvels of art of the world.

Mr. Leland, as we have said, was greatly interested in humane and

INTERIOR OF A PALACE, SEVILLE.

missionary efforts. When a traveller visits a new city, he always seeks to find there *himself*, or some expression of his own thoughts, views, and purposes. Thus travellers see many different cities in the same city, and Mr. Leland found in Seville what few other transient visitors would have so readily seen.

### HIS OWN GHOST. — DON JUAN.

"I have always been interested," said Mr. Leland, in giving an account of an incident at Seville, "in the cure of a malady that is worse than any form of physical disease. It is the misfortune of a depraved imagination and a will weakened by sin. Friends have said to me, 'When a man's will power is gone, the man is lost.' I have always pitied the morally diseased, and have always been intensely interested in cases of moral recovery, and have asked myself, 'Is the will power ever lost?'

"Before I left America, while waiting for the sailing of the ship from New York, I attended a funeral such as that great city had never seen before. It was a golden September day. The church in which the services were to be held was crowded. The streets in the vicinity were filled with waiting people.

"In the great throng that crowded church and street were ministers, philanthropists, merchants, thieves, confidence men, women with painted faces, children in rags. Before the pulpit, amid the sweetness of flowers, lay the dead form of a man who was once a river-thief. On the black drapery of the wall back of the pulpit were these words, the last words of him whose life the crowd had come to honor, —

"'It is all right!'

"At the age of thirteen this man had landed from an emigrant ship in the great, crowded, wicked city. Alone in the wilderness of homes, he made the acquaintance and friendship of the low, the idle, and the vicious. He became a prize-fighter, a drunkard, a river-thief, and for his crimes was sentenced to Sing Sing.

"But the life he led troubled his conscience. Weary and sick of sin, he sought to escape it. In his seeking he found good men ready to help him. Soon there sprung up in his heart an almost patriarchal faith, — a faith that the Spirit of God was able to change his sinful nature; that a new life, through a spiritual renewal, was possible to him.

"His faith had saved him. It saved others. He established a mission in the most criminal and dangerous part of the city, and began to preach there the one doctrine of moral recovery through acceptance of a divine Master and an inward experience of the Spirit of God.

"Year by year the work went on. Some of the most abandoned criminals were led to give themselves to this man's Master and to enter upon the new life. These experiences multiplied, and became an influence. People wondered at its power. The story of the mission of Jerry McAuley filled the city and the country. The mission itself became a monument of faith.

"And so on that calm September day thoughtful men gathered among the most depraved people, to respect the memory of the dead river-thief.

"Faith has her conquests, age by age; and such a man is a conqueror. Tears fell like rain on his grave, and thousands of silent hearts and prayers pronounced over it their benedictions, and thus testified to the power of his life.

"I was deeply interested in this case. I thought of it often on the voyage, and as often asked myself, 'Is this faith possible to all?'

"On arriving at Seville, I visited the Cathedral, heard its great organ of five thousand pipes, and then inquired for the Charity Hospital, which I had been told was one of the most creditable monuments of the heart of the beautiful city.

"I had heard also of the wonderful paintings of this place; and the indefinite information that I had acquired, led me to search for the facts of its origin and history.

"A strange character was revealed to me, — one that I had known through poetry, romance, and music, since I was a child, but the true lesson of whose life I had never seen clearly until now.

"It was Don Juan.

"I had always associated the name with that of a gay rake, and not with a redeemed and transfigured life.

"There lived in Seville, about the year 1671, a most profligate man by the name of Don Miguel de Manara Vecentello de Leca. He was a slave of his evil passions, an evil influence wherever he appeared; fascinating the young by his beauty, gayety, and display of wealth, and heartlessly alluring them to ruin. He was given the name of Don Juan.

"One night, according to the received story, he left a scene of debauchery at a late hour, to return to his home. He was alone, and the streets were silent. The night was mild; a dim moon shone on the Guadalquivir, — the purple-silver moonlight of Andalusia.

THE ROCK OF GIBRALTAR.

"There was something alarming to him in the silence of the city, something awful to him in the thought of his being alone.

"A strange power seemed to control him. Suddenly everything about him appeared to change, and his life to pass into a vision.

"In the street rose a shadowy procession. It consisted of monks, of the

THE FUNERAL PROCESSION.

order of the Brothers of Compassion. The forms were ghostly and silent. They were bearing a body to burial.

"Whose, in silence and the night? What frail life had been so hopelessly bad as to invite oblivion before the body had been covered by the grave?

"His curiosity was excited. He hurried past the shadowy and silent forms, and stood by the bier, his heart throbbing in pity for the life that had gone out so hopelessly.

"He drew the covering from the bier. The moonlight fell upon the face of the dead. He knew the man, and started back.

"Was it some victim that he had brought to ruin? No; the dead face on the bier was that of *himself*.

"The procession passed on, bearing himself. He followed it, his only mourner.

"On, on it went toward the Potter's Field. Don Miguel began inwardly to pray to be delivered from himself.

"The vision faded; but it had wrought a complete change in the desires, purposes, and character of the man.

"His one question now was, 'Is there any good thing possible to a character like mine?'

"He possessed a great fortune. This he at once consecrated to the purpose of founding a hospital for the poor.

"He was a lover of art, and this passion he also resolved to change from evil into good. He employed the greatest painters among them, Murillo — to adorn the new hospital. It rose a treasure-house of art above the Guadalquivir, and stands crowned to-day among the most useful and invaluable institutions of Spain."

From Seville Mr. Leland and Charlie went to Granada, and thence to Gibraltar, where they were to find the steamer.

We cannot give space to this Spanish journey. The father and son could but remember the works of Irving, and pity the fate of Boabdil the Unlucky, as they turned away from beautiful Granada, and were carried by a swifter steed than the Moorish monarch's toward the sea.

At Gibraltar the Mediterranean lay before them, foaming in wintry restlessness; and beyond lay the coast of Africa.

Visions of the east began to rise even here. Along the cloudy shores in the dim distance marched the armies of Hamilcar, of the Hasdrubals, and of Hannibal. The proud navies of Carthage here rode upon the sea.

The story of Dido came back like a dream: the sudden rise of Carthage, and the hostility of the city to Rome.

HANNIBAL SWEARING ETERNAL HATRED TO THE ROMANS

Then, in a vision, the conquest of Spain by the new city of Afric; the First Punic War; the defeat of the Carthaginians by the Romans.

HANNIBAL ON AN EXPEDITION.

Hamilcar brings his young son Hannibal to the sacred altar, and compels the boy to swear eternal hatred to the Romans.

The boy aspires to humble Rome. How? By the way of Spain.

He comes to manhood. His army clouds the African coast, and his navy darkens the sea.

From Carthage to Spain he begins a march in which he is to ascend to the clouds on the stairs of the Alps, and thence descend to Italy like a thunderbolt; from Spain to Gaul; from Gaul to the Alps; up the Alps to the sky; from the sky to the glowing provinces of Rome.

Over this sea, too, departed Boabdil the Unfortunate, the last of the Moors, when Spain reconquered Granada, and won a throne that was not to limit its power to Andalusia, but to carry it to a new world, and there plant the banners of Aragon and Castile.

### TOWARD THE SEA.

There was weeping in Granada on that eventful day:
One king in triumph entered in; one vanquished rode away.
Down from the Alhambra's minarets was every crescent flung,
And the cry of "Santiago!" through the jewelled palace rung.
  And singing, singing, singing,
  Were the nightingales of Spain :
  But the Moorish monarch, lonely,
  The cadences heard only.
  "They sadly sing," said he ;
  "They sadly sing to me."
  And through the groves melodious
  He rode toward the sea.

There was joy in old Granada on that eventful day:
One king in triumph entered in ; one slowly rode away.
Up the Alcala singing marched the gay cavaliers ;
Gained was the Moslem empire of twice three hundred years.
  And singing, singing, singing,
  Were the nightingales of Spain ;
  But the Moorish monarch, lonely,
  The cadences heard only.
  "They sadly sing," said he ;
  "They sadly sing to me,
  All the birds of Andalusia!"
  And he rode toward the sea.

## TO THE MEDITERRANEAN.

Through the groves of Alpuxarrus, on that eventful day,
The vanquished king rode slowly and tearfully away.
He paused upon the Xenil, and saw Granada fair
Wreathed with the sunset's roses in palpitating air.
  And singing, singing, singing,
  Were the nightingales of Spain,
  But the Moorish monarch, lonely,
  The cadences heard only.
  "They sadly sing," said he ;
  " They sadly sing to me,
  The groves of Andalusia ! "
  He rode toward the sea.

The Verga heaped with flowers below the city lay,
And faded in the sunset, as he slowly rode away ;
And he paused again a moment amid the cavaliers,
And saw the golden palace shine through the mist of tears.
  And singing, singing, singing,
  Were the nightingales of Spain ;
  But the Moorish monarch, lonely,
  The cadences heard only.
  " They sadly sing," said he ;
  " They sadly sing to me :
  Farewell, O Andalusia ! "
  And he rode toward the sea.

Past the gardens of Granada rode Isabella fair,
As twilight's parting roses fell on the sea of air :
She heard the lisping fountains, and not the Moslem's sighs :
She saw the sun-crowned mountains, and not the tear-wet eyes.
  " Sing on," she said, " forever,
  O nightingales of Spain !
  Xenil nor Guadalquivir
  Will *he* ne'er see again.
  Ye sweetly sing," said she,
  " Ye sweetly sing to me."
  *She* rode toward the palace ;
  *He* rode toward the sea.

# CHAPTER VI.

### TO THE PYRAMIDS.

ALEXANDRIA. — CAIRO. — STORY OF SESOSTRIS. — THE MYSTERIOUS PILGRIMS.

Over the winter sea to Majorca, — an island lovely at all seasons of the year, bright in the light of a sky of eternal blue, and warm in the air of eternal spring; thence to Genoa, — Genoa the superb, — presenting to the seer a picture as of hills white with palaces; to Malta, where we would love to linger and recall the romances of the Knights of St. John; thence to Alexandria, the last part of the voyage in view of the African coast.

The incidents of this voyage alone might fill a book. They filled a month in time; for the steamer remained some days at each port. At Genoa our tourists made an excursion to Geneva, a car-ride of only about fourteen hours, and beheld the winter Alps. At Malta they visited the ruined fortresses of what was one of the most powerful and romantic orders of knighthood of the Middle Ages.

They approached the Greek city of Alexandria at nightfall, but did not land in the night. A lighthouse threw its rays into the darkness of the March night; but it was not the famous Pharos of old, which was four hundred feet high, and blazed like a star over the city and sea for sixteen hundred years, and was esteemed one of the wonders of the world.

In the morning Alexandria, the gate of Egypt, was full in view, — to all outward appearance a European city, excepting the slender minarets, whose arms seemed reaching to heaven.

"Egypt!" said Mr. Leland to Charlie.

"What do we owe to Egypt?" asked Charlie, whose Western training made him practical in the very sight of the land of stupendous mysteries.

"She nurtured the Hebrew race in its infancy; to the Hebrews we owe the development of moral truth."

"Yes."

"She educated Moses, the moral law-giver of the world."

"Yes."

"Christ himself was cradled in Egypt, and Christianity in its childhood was educated in the Greek schools of Alexandria."

"She has been a kind of foster-mother," said Charlie.

"St. Mark carried the Gospel to Alexandria, and Egypt was the first nation in the world to accept Christianity."

"Do you suppose that we shall find the old interpreter Ali Bedair on the quay?"

"Yes!" said Mr. Leland, confidently; "he will be the first to greet us."

Mr. Leland was right. On the landing stood the tall patriarchal form of the old interpreter, and near him three young men were waving white handkerchiefs. Who could they be?

"Frank Gray," said Charlie, as the boat drew near, — "Frank Gray, from Athens; Wyllys Winn, from London; and — Charlie Noble, I do believe! What but a desire to see the world could have sent him here? I am glad to see one face from Boston. He is the $500 boy."

## ALEXANDRIA. — CAIRO. — THE GREAT PYRAMID.

"My father will leave nothing for me to do," said the boy Alexander, as he counted the conquests of his father Philip of Macedon.

The boy fed his imagination on the Iliad; and a boy's life usually follows the courses of the heroes about whom he loves best to read.

Alexander conquered the world, and died at thirty-two. He left Persepolis, the wonder of Asia, in ashes; but he founded Alexandria, and there his body found rest at last in a coffin of gold.

The conquests of Alexander filled the world with the thought and the literature of Greece. Alexandria became a favorite resort of the Greeks, and the literary and ecclesiastical centre of Greek literature, — the new Athens of the Eastern World. It was the Greek capital of conquered Egypt, the mistress of the Nile, the crowned city of the arts and arms of the Mediterranean. It was founded in the autumn of B.C. 332.

Before it rose the Pharos, the star of the sea. Its streets were long colonnades; its library, the greatest of ancient times.

The ancient city is dead, and buried deep amid the sands of the Nile. The so-called Pompey's Pillar is its solitary monument. The picturesque city of to-day has few connecting links with the past. It has nearly a quarter of a million of inhabitants; and more than four thousand ships drop their anchors yearly in its harbor.

ALEXANDER THE GREAT.

Our tourists spent one night at Alexandria, at the Hotel Abbat. In the morning they left the city of the Ptolemies for Cairo, by the railway that connects the two cities, intending to spend some days here on their return.

"It seems indeed strange to be travelling in cars in Egypt," said Charlie.

"Why?" asked his father.

"There is something unhistorical about it. Look at those Arabian guards and porters dressed like Englishmen. How much was the fare?"

"About four dollars, second class."

"Travelling from the city of the Ptolemies to grand Cairo and the Pyramids on an English railway-carriage, with guards in English clothes; second class; fare about four dollars — I never dreamed of Egypt in that way; it seems to me ridiculous."

Our tourists had taken a lunch with them from Alexandria. When they had finished eating, the descendants of the subjects of the Ptolemies gathered around them with mournful faces to beg what was left. This was not poetry. Our tourists had seen but little poetry in Egypt thus far, except the flower-carpeted fields, and the deep liquid blue of the sky.

The white city of minarets at length rose under the celestial blue, a picture standing against the gold curtains of the air. Donkeys, instead of horse-cars or cabs, were waiting to take them to the hotel, or wherever they might wish to go.

The Pyramids, like piles of gloom, rose in sight amid the dusky gold of the afternoon air. The boys were impatient to go to them at once. These structures had filled their dreams with wonder; and now that they rose before their very vision, they could not help exclaiming, —

"Donkeys for the Pyramids."

"If you cannot wait, go," said Mr. Leland. "I cannot go now; I must make an arrangement for a dahabieh [Nile boat] for Thebes, and a dragoman to take charge of us and our journey."

The boys were told by the Arabs that it would take but four or five hours to visit the Pyramids, and the story seemed plausible. It was now getting somewhat late in the day for the journey.

If our young tourists were disappointed in their first impressions of Egypt, all was changed as they went out of Cairo. The city itself at a little distance seemed unreal, — a picture on the air, a vision, a poem. The minarets of Cairo are the most beautiful in the Levant. They are of immense height, slender, and graceful, and beautiful in the alternating colors of red and white stone.

The Pyramids! There were three, but the largest was so gigantic as to draw the eye wholly to itself. It seemed to grow until it shut out the sky. The Arabs chattered indifferently as they approached it, but the boys were silent. There was something that closed their lips in the awe-inspiring presence of this ancient monster of stone.

This Pyramid — the tomb of Cheops, also called the Great Pyramid — must have been between three or four thousand years old when the Star led the Magi to Bethlehem, and the Gospel brought new light to mankind. It is higher than the dome of St. Paul's Cathedral, and its base is some seven hundred and sixty-four feet square. The tomb-chamber is reached by a passage three hundred and twenty feet long. It required the work of one hundred thousand men for thirty, and, according to some archæologists, fifty years, to bring its immense angles to the apex, and thus complete this the most stupendous tomb ever erected by human hands.

The face of the Pyramid, which at a little distance appeared like a smooth inclined surface, suddenly changed. It now seemed to be an immense staircase, a threshold to the sky.

"Up?" asked the Arabs.

"Can we go up?"

"Up," said the Arabs, pointing skyward.

AN EGYPTIAN VILLA.

The boys pointed up. They were seized by the hands of their Arab guides, and pulled upward, step over step. They stood on the last steps at last, and before them lay Egypt in the blaze of the late afternoon, airy Cairo, the Nile, the lesser Pyramids, and the Sphinx. They were standing on the tomb of a monarch who ruled in the infancy of the world.

BRICK PYRAMID OF FAIOUM.

Darkness came on suddenly after the sunset. When the boys returned to Cairo, a new wonder made them feel as though they were in Europe again: the streets were lighted with gas.

The next day, in the care of Ali Bedair the Interpreter, the whole party visited the Sphinx.

The boys had asked to be called early in the morning. They need hardly have made the request. They were awakened by human voices that seemed like bells in the air, saying, as translated into English, —

"God is God. Prayer is better than sleep. Allah! Allah! Allah!"

It was a voice from the minaret.

"God is God, — there is no God but God."

As the boys stepped out of Shepheard's Hotel, a novel sight awaited them. There were eight or more Arabs, with sleepy little donkeys, all of them urging with the utmost vehemence an English lady and gentleman to employ them. Their attention was at once turned to the new party; and their faces lighted up with expectation when they saw that it consisted largely of boys.

Presently Ali Bedair appeared, and addressed to them a few mysterious words. The noise subsided; and soon the party, on six little donkeys, were on their way towards the Sphinx.

The rising sun shone full in the face of the wonder, as it had done for thousands of years. But for its chipped face, the head would have been as beautiful as it was majestic. The sand had been dug away from its pedestal, like the throwing aside of a garment.

"What was the Sphinx?" asked Wyllys Winn of Ali Bedair.

"What is the Sphinx?" asked Charlie at the same time.

The others made inquiries by looks, and waited for an answer.

"A lion with the head of a woman, my boys."

"Who made it?"

"A Pharaoh."

"Why?"

DONKEY BOYS.

has been waiting for the dawn. Mornings have come and mornings have gone, and blessed mankind, but still she watches. She said to old Egypt what the Book of Job said to the Hebrews: 'The world knows nothing, God rules for the best; trust and be silent.'"

"Was the Sphinx a goddess?" asked Charlie.

"No; a god."

"With a woman's head?"

"Yes. Harmachis."

"Who was Harmachis?"

"Horas on the horizon." He added, sagely: "Light conquers darkness; it is an emblem of the power that overcomes sin and death. The Sphinx was erected as a temple of the Light,— the Dawning of Day."

"A temple?" asked Charlie.

"Yes. In the ages long ago, innumerable worshippers at sunrise ascended the steps to an altar that stood on an inlaid pavement between the mighty paws of the giant. The sky flashed and flamed. The darkness became thin, and rolled away. Then the sun blazed on Egypt, and here rose the chants of the forgotten priests of lost temples and palaces. The Sphinx was the idol of the Rising Sun."

Such was the old man's view. It was poetic and fitted the hour, and the boys were pleased to accept it. It is the view that is generally received.

The figure once stood high above the sands. It measures some sixty-four feet from the crown of the head to the paws, but its pedestal is largely buried in the sand.

Before we proceed farther with our narrative, it may be well to give some account of Egypt's greatest hero, whose name is associated with her most stupendous monuments.

## SESOSTRIS.

Among the earliest conquerors of the world was Sesostris, or Rameses the Great. His fame once awed the nations, and his name still leads the records on the crumbling monuments of Egypt. He is often spoken of in history as Rameses II., and sometimes as Rameses-Sesostris.

His youth was heroic, and he was educated to ambition. It was the purpose of his father to train his son to be a conqueror. It was a period of grand dynasties ; Egypt was the queen of nations, and the house of Rameses seemed to have dreamed that this boy would one day win universal empire, and chain the captives of all nations to his car of triumph.

The boy inherited the ambitions of his ancestors. In his eye conquest was glory ; he hoped one day to fill the world with the fame of his splendid achievements in arts and arms, and write his name on monuments that would never perish.

His father ordered that all the male children that were born on the same day as his son, should be brought to the palace and educated with him in heroic exercises. When asked in regard to his reason for granting his son so many companions, he would answer, —

"That they may be true to him in war."

The old Egyptian placed a high value on the power of youthful friendship, and his judgment proved to be correct.

So Sesostris grew up amid noble friendships, in a school of heroes. Egypt now was a nation of palaces and treasure-houses. The air was darkened by stupendous monuments, and gorgeous and sublime rituals filled the temples of the gods.

When Sesostris and his young friends came to manhood, the monarch sent them at the head of an army into Arabia to test the results of their martial training. Sesostris and his young generals conquered Arabia. The old monarch then sent them into Western Africa on a like expedition. They subdued the West, and returned in triumph.

Sesostris ascended the throne. He divided Egypt into thirty-six provinces, and appointed a governor over each, and then began to make preparations to fulfil the dream of his ancestors, and make Egypt the mistress of the world.

He began to gather his army. It was a dark, glittering, fearful host. His war-chariots numbered twenty-seven thousand ; his foot-soldiers six hundred

PYRAMIDS AND SPHINX.

thousand. His fleet, which he brought into line on the shores of the Red Sea, consisted of four hundred ships.

Now he and his young warriors swept forth from the Nile, and began to shatter the affrighted armies that gathered to oppose them. Sesostris con-

RAMESES.

quered Ethiopia, then all Asia to the Ganges ; he then crossed over to Europe, and made a conquest of Thrace.

Wherever he went, Sesostris left the monuments of his conquests and glory ; these were called Stelæ. They were pillars of stone, simple, but as he supposed imperishable ; and all of them were made to testify to the unwilling nations the power of Rameses. His army moved on, desolating the world for nine years, leaving the stelæ behind them.

The triumph of Sesostris, on his return to Egypt, was the greatest of ancient times. The captives of all nations were chained to his triumphal car. He had robbed the world of treasures, and he brought back a great army of slaves.

Having conquered the world, it was now his ambition to fill Egypt with temples, palaces, and monuments. Gigantic structures arose, and Thebes became the wonder of the world, and the monument of his achievements.

MEDINET. COURT OF RAMESES.

Amid all this success and temporal splendor, his eyes began to grow dim. He could no longer see, as of old, the monuments and their inscriptions, the temples and the palaces. The world grew dark to him, — the light of day, and the glories of the land to which he had given his life and his heart.

Sesostris became blind.

His proud spirit and imperious self-will could not endure the misfortune and humiliation. Was fate stronger than the spirit that had subdued the world? Could calamity find him, and circumstance bind him, like a common man?

TRIUMPHAL CAR OF SESOSTRIS.

The world was lost to him now, all dark, and he no longer desired to live. What was all the winged glory of Egypt to a king without eyes?

Sesostris ended his life by his own hand, after a long reign of sixty-six years.

The earth has swallowed up the stelae that marked his triumphal marches. They are gone from Syria, Ionia, and Thrace. Thebes is dust. The morning Memnon is dead to the ear of the world. The name of Rameses is indeed found on the ruins of the stupendous monuments of the period of Egypt's splendor and power, but it is the adornment of broken columns or crumbling stone. The traveller reads it with the reflection that the imperishable temples and palaces and monuments of life are not material things, but structures of the soul. The simple philosophy of Paul, in his poverty, humiliation, and wanderings, outweighs them all: "The things that are unseen are eternal."

## THE MYSTERIOUS PILGRIMS.

Ancient Memphis beheld the sun rise and set on the Pyramids for four thousand years. The city is now a graveyard; nought remains but her monuments.

Cairo, that succeeded Memphis, though built on the other side of the Nile, is a child among the Egyptian cities; a child in age, in stature, in thought, in development and achievement.

Nearly nineteen hundred years ago, when ancient Memphis was still in her magnificence, a pilgrim family came travelling towards the Nile. It consisted of a patriarchal man, a virgin, and an infant child.

It had long been prophesied that one day a Child would be born of a Virgin, that his advent should be made known by a Star, and that when this event should take place, the sun-gods of Egypt should crumble and fall.

"A Star shall rise out of Jacob," said the Hebrew seer.

"A Star shall rise out of Jacob," said Zoroaster.

The Magi had watched and waited for the rising of that Star for a thousand years.

The pilgrims journeyed by night. They came from Bethlehem, the ancient home of Benjamin, of Ruth and David. They may have passed the tomb of the patriarchs, at Hebron, and trod in the ways over which Moses led their ancestors in ever memorable days.

Quietly they came to the Nile, and found protection in the city in the shadows of the Pyramids.

The Nile was lovely then. Its fields were paved with the lotus; it fed and perfumed Rome with roses, and the fruits of the world burdened its banks.

The patriarch and the Virgin did not announce whence they came, or why, or whither they were going.

They bore with them an infant King. The Child slept in the shadows of the Pyramids; and Memphis from that time began to crumble, as the seers had foretold. Yet Egypt did not know when it came or when it departed, or that the perfumes of the lilies of the Nile had been breathed by One who was to set up a spiritual kingdom that should fill the world, and grow, when Memphis was dust.

The pilgrims may have tarried here three years. They silently came, lived in silence, and as silently went away. The earliest objects to fill the eyes of the Child with wonder must have been the Pyramids.

The Child grew. He preached a new gospel of salvation, and gave his life for men. He ascended to heaven, having declared to his followers that he would reign forever through the Holy Spirit.

Egypt, that was the first nation to receive and shelter him, was the first to receive and shelter his Gospel. She had prepared herself, by the monuments of four thousand years, to believe the doctrines of a re-creation of the spirit in divine love, and the immortality of the soul.

Then Egypt ceased to build temples with hands. The people's minds were turned to the temples of the soul. Cities of gold and crystal arose, but they were invisible. Yet they live, and shall live when the Pyramids shall have crumbled forever, and the world itself have changed.

MEDINET. TEMPLE-PALACE OF RAMESES.

## CHAPTER VII.

#### THE RUINS OF THE QUEEN CITY OF THE WORLD.

##### ON THE NILE. — KARNAK.

HE next day our tourists started for Thebes on one of those floating homes called a Nile boat, and in the charge of a dragoman to whom had been intrusted all the provisions for the journey and the care of the party to Karnak. They expected to return more quickly by a steamer.

The Nile boat is a peculiar craft, long and narrow, with saloons in the after part and ample awnings over the deck. It will comfortably accommodate some six or eight people. It has arrangements for both sails and oars, is usually well stored with provisions, and a party may drift in it for days, leading a dreamy, lazy life, with the most stupendous ruins coming into view or fading from it, cool palms and shadowy camels in the clear distances, a sky all splendor above, and beauty everywhere.

The boat is tied up to some object on the shore at night, as though it were a horse or a cow. There is little danger to the travellers thus exposed.

Night on the Nile is a magnificence unknown to the West. Suddenly after sunset the deep shadow falls; brilliant stars come out and seem to drop low, like lamps in a mighty palace; the rising moon is like another sun; the soft air is a deep-sea splendor, and there are a hush and a silence on every hand that invite adoration and rest.

In the morning the air is filled with birds. European travellers, who place less value on animal life and have less heart in this respect than the Arabs, shoot at the birds for sport, and smile without compunction of conscience as they see the poor creatures with broken wings tumbling down from the heights of the air.

## SCAVENGER BIRDS.

It is said that but for the scavenger birds the lands of the tropics and the South could not be inhabited. "If they failed for a single day," is the strong language of Michelet, "the country would become a desert."

In indolent Africa thousands of villages depend upon them for purification. In drowsy America south of Panama or Caracas, they, swiftest of cleansers, must sweep out and purify the town before the Spaniard rises, ere the sun has stirred the carcass and the mass of offal into fermentation.

These scavengers are found in all the warm countries of the earth. When it is evening-time in America, and the urubu, his day's work ended, replaces himself in the cocoanut tree, the minarets of Asia sparkle in the morning rays. Not less faithful than their American brothers, vultures, crows, storks, ibises, set out from their balconies on their various missions, — some to the fields, to destroy the insect and the serpent; others, alighting in the streets of Alexandria and Cairo, hasten to accomplish their task of municipal scavengering. Did they take the briefest holiday, the plague would soon be the only inhabitant of the country.

Thus, in the two hemispheres, the great work of public health is performed with solemn and wonderful regularity. If the sun is punctual in fertilizing life, these scavengers are no less punctual in withdrawing from his rays the shocking spectacle of death.

Seemingly, they are not ignorant of the importance of their functions. Approach them, and they will not retreat. When they have received the signal from their comrades, the crows, which precede them and point out their prey,

DUCK SHOOTING ON THE NILE.

you will see the vultures descend in a cloud from one knows not whence, as if from heaven.

Naturally solitary, and without communication, — mostly silent, — they flock to the banquet by the hundred, and nothing disturbs them. They never quarrel among themselves, and they take no heed of the passer-by. They imperturbably accomplish their functions with a stern gravity, with decency and propriety; the corpse disappears, the skin remains. In a moment, as it were, a mass of animal matter that would soon be putrid fermentation has vanished.

It is strange that the more odious they are to us, the more useful we find them. They always seem hungry, and wear a hungry expression. Let them devour a hippopotamus, and they still seem to be famishing. To the gulls, those multitudinous vultures of the sea, a whale seems but a reasonable morsel. As long as aught of it remains, they remain; fire at them, and they return to it in the very mouth of your guns. Nothing dislodges the vulture on the carcass of a hippopotamus.

Devaillant killed one of these birds, which, when mortally wounded, still plucked away scraps of flesh. Was he starving? Not he. Food was found in his stomach weighing six pounds!

Standing before them, you feel yourself in the presence of the ministers of death; but of death tranquil and natural, and not of murder. They are the agents of a beneficent chemistry, that preserves the balances of life here below. They labor for us in a thousand places where we ourselves may never penetrate. We can clearly see their services in the town, but no one can measure the full extent of their benefits in those deserts where the winds are laden with the poison of death.

In the fathomless forest, in the deep morasses, under the impure shadow of mangoes and mangroves, where ferment the corpses of two worlds, dashed to and fro by the sea, the great purifying army goes on the wings of air; and woe to the inhabited world if their mysterious and unknown toil should cease for an instant!

In America these benefactors are protected by law. Egypt does more for them: she reveres and loves them. The ancient worship of these birds no longer exists, but they still receive the same hospitality in the regions of the Nile and the desert as in the time of Pharaoh. Ask an Egyptian fellah why he allows himself to be infested and deafened by birds; why he endures the insolence of the crow, posted on his buffalo's horn or his camel's hump. He will answer nothing. To the bird everything is lawful. He knows that man lives only through the instrumentality of his winged protector.

The universal sympathy of man with the harmless species of the animal kingdom is one of the charms of the East. The West has its peculiar splendors; but the moral attraction of Asia, with all her ignorance and superstition, lies in the unity between man and Nature, — where the primitive alliance remains unbroken, where the animals are ignorant that they have cause to dread the human species.

There is a gentle pleasure in observing this confidence between man and the birds, in seeing the inhabitants of the air come at the Brahmin's call to eat out of his hand.

"At Cairo," says a traveller, "the level roofs of the houses are covered by a crowd of birds. Even the eagles sleep on the balconies of the minarets."

Conquerors from the West have never failed to turn into derision and ridicule this gentleness for animated Nature; but destroy these animals, and the country would be no longer habitable. That which has saved India and Egypt through so many misfortunes, and preserved their fertility, is neither the Nile nor the Ganges, but the respect for animal life, the mildness and the gentle heart of man.

We have followed the thought of Michelet, which we recalled with gratitude here, where the air was swarming with beneficent wings.

The cool north winds blow the sails that move up the Nile during the winter, and temper the warm spring air. The sunrise and sunsets glimmer with the wings of birds. The waters are calm, except in eddies, or when disturbed by squalls after dark.

## THE COPTS.

The Nile is made interesting to the American Christian from its associations with Coptic traditions and events.

Who are the Copts?

They are the descendants of the early Christians. They number about one hundred and fifty thousand.

Egypt was the first nation to receive the Gospel. St. Mark was her missionary preacher. It is related that he fell a martyr to the

VULTURES IN EGYPT.

cause in Alexandria; that he was tied to a cart and dragged over the pavements of the streets until life was nearly extinct; that then he was thrown into a cave to die, where Christ appeared to him in a vision. He was buried in Alexandria; but his body after a time was removed to Venice, and the Cathedral of St. Mark, a pile of gems, — the beautiful stones of all lands, — was erected as his memorial.

The Coptic church, or Jewish and Greek church, thus founded by St. Mark at Alexandria, carried the Gospel into all Egypt. Christianity here established her schools. Great men arose; among them, Clement of Alexandria, Athanasius, Origen, now among the most esteemed of the Church fathers. The Church had a period of glory, but declined after the conquest of Egypt by the Mohammedans.

The Copts injured their cause by not following the examples of St. Mark and St. Paul. Instead of sending forth missionaries, as did Rome, to convert the world, they favored cloister life, hermitages, and retirement from the world. The Nile is full of ruined monasteries. Caves of anchorites are everywhere to be found. It is said that at one time there were one hundred thousand Coptic recluses in Egypt, and that fifty thousand hermits at this period once came out of their hermitages and caves to attend an Easter festival at Tabenna. The fruit of this secluded and barren life was small; it is missionary activity that produces results.

No road could be like the Nile. The objects on the shore seem to move slowly, but the boat does not. Life is all a dream.

The city of Sioot came into the vision, white minarets against a dark background of Libyan mountains. The banks were filled with flowers of every hue; the winds bore delicate perfumes on their light wings.

Again and again herds of buffalo and other animals were seen rushing down to the river, then drinking, then plunging in, and disappearing from sight.

Ducks fill the still water, and melons line the banks. The people put melons over their heads, having made eye-holes in them, and swim among the ducks as though their heads were floating melons, and so capture the poor birds at will.

Day by day passed in this atmosphere of luxury.

But grand sights are at hand. The ghosts of Thebes already shadow the distance.

"Karnak!" said the dragoman, shading his eyes with his hand.

All was expectation. The most stupendous structures of human art were darkening the bright air, — the ruined temples of vanished gods, and the crumbling palaces of men who were once deemed divine.

The Temple Palace of Karnak was the grandest structure of human thought and hands. Godlike minds planned it, to which the architects of to-day are as pygmies; armies of builders carried out the gigantic plan. It was twelve hundred feet long. St. Peter's at Rome, the greatest structure of the present time, might have been a porch to it. The famous cathedral at Cologne might have been set down in its Hypostyle Hall.

The ruins of Thebes cover an area of many miles, and the Nile flows silently through them. On one side of the river is the so-called Thebes; on the other, Karnak and Luxor. All was once Thebes; it is a village of beggarly showmen now, a plain filled with ruins and flowers.

## THEBES BY DAY.

The approach to the ruins of Thebes is somewhat disappointing. The historic city rises in a vision; and instead of the half-expected grandeur there are airy ruins and vacancy. After passing lateen sails on the river, and curious pigeon towers along the banks, tombs of Coptic saints, caverns of dust of men and animals once regarded sacred, clumps of palms and shapeless mud huts, the Ramesuem, and

FALLS OF THE NILE.

COPTIC MAIDEN.

the two colossi appear; and one gazes into vacant air full of peace and sunshine.

The Libyan hills, which have had the charm of a far-off picturesqueness, draw near, then sweep away again. The Arabian hills present the same feature; and between them both at last opens a great area or plain, such as a king might choose for the founding of a splendid city. As the boat drifts on, here rises a broken pylon, there a crumbling obelisk. The plain, with its rampart of cliffs, comes into nearer view.

Some twenty ruins of temples remain on the plain, and the outline of no ruin is entire. Karnak is a pile of broken columns; only a small part of the Ramescum remains; the two sentinel colossi alone recall the glory of the once stupendous temple of Amenoph.

The plain is a graveyard. Monuments and halls of the dead alone remain. Thebes was not built to endure. "Life is but for a moment," said the ancient priests of the sun. "Hurry to build your tomb; you are but dwellers in tents, but the soul may need the old home of the body again; preserve it; care for the soul is the only care worth heeding; this life is dust."

They were men of mighty thought, those old builders. They worshipped Amor, and built colossal tombs. Human life and force for ages spent themselves in the building of tombs. Generation followed generation, and each generation was employed in building its own tombs; and so the centuries moved on.

The temples on the Libyan side of the old city are entrances to the chambers of the dead.

One of the first visits of our tourists was to the Ramescum, or the Temple of Rameses II. (Sesostris), which has been already spoken of; and to the colossi, which have been described.

The next journey was to the great temple of Rameses III. at Medinet Abo. The second night of the visit was passed in a tomb whose tenant had long ago turned to dust, and needed it no longer. The last day was spent at Luxor.

The door of the tomb where the second night was passed commanded a view of nearly the whole plain.

KARNAK, HYPOSTYLE HALL.

The plain was yellow and green; palm-trees nodded in the light Nile winds, and ghosts of palaces everywhere appeared. The visitors

KARNAK, EXTERIOR WALL.

encountered bats in the ruins; and Arab boys with donkeys came to visit them, and argued in an unknown tongue with Ali Bedair.

Some of these Arab boys were very handsome. They seemed to have no ambition except for the day; wherever our tourists met them they were quick to devise excuses for asking for money, but beyond this they appeared to be lost in contemplation.

"What do the young Arabs constantly meditate upon?" asked Charlie of the interpreter.

"Nothing, my son," was the reply.

Thebes by day! We must let the pencil of the artist bring it into view. No description can equal the artist's work; and that work is so faithfully done that you would recognize every feature of it if you found yourself a pilgrim alone on the plain of Thebes.

## QUEEN HATASU.

In the temple of Karnak a tall monolith awakened the curiosity of the visitors.

"What is its history?" asked Charlie Noble of the interpreter.

"Queen Hatasu, daughter of Thothmes I.," answered the interpreter.

"Her monument?"

"No; she built her monument out of a mountain. She caused the monolith to be erected, as a work of beauty and art."

"Who was she?"

"She was a person who had the form of a woman, but the spirit of a man. She was one of the master-builders of Thebes.

"She ordered the people to regard her as a man, and to call her *King*. She filled the city with her pictures and statues, and is everywhere represented as a king with a full beard. So, whenever you find a picture of a queen with a beard, and the head-dress of a king, you may suppose that it is Queen Hatasu."

On the road from Luxor to Karnak our travellers met a dealer in antiquities, and purchased some specimens similar to those so well

COURT OF THE COLOSSI.

displayed in the Boston Art Museum. The dealer was found sitting between two sphinxes, one of them having the head of a woman and the other of a goat. His " bazaar " was a simple carpet or rug spread upon the ground.

## THE SACRED CAT.

Egypt is the land of cats. " If I wanted a good cat, I would go to Egypt," said an old traveller. The cats were once regarded as sacred, and cat-headed images everywhere appear. The cat was the emblem of affection, — Aphrodite. There were once held in Egypt festivals of cats, that called together each some seven hundred thousand pilgrims.

In the great pilgrimages to Mecca a camel loaded with cats in baskets, under the care of a venerable follower of the Prophet, is still a conspicuous object; for customs do not always change the history or religion of a country. If the cat is no longer held sacred as the emblem of a daughter of the sun, she is still regarded as one of the most precious blessings of the land of the lotus, and nothing handsomer than an Egyptian kitten is to be seen in the animal kingdom.

" Do you wonder that they used to worship cats?" asked Charlie of Charlie, as they saw a group of these beauties purring in the sun.

" Egypt must have been a paradise for old women and children," was the answer.

At Karnak there was a temple that contained more than five hundred cat-headed statues. They were made of black granite, and were somewhat like the cat-headed statue in the Boston Museum of Fine Arts. A number of these grotesque figures can still be seen near an ancient tank. Charlie Noble and Charlie Leland went to look at them by moonlight, under the guidance of Ali Bedair.

" It was *awful!* " was the report of one Charlie; and the other Charlie, using a Shakspearean double superlative, declared, " It was the most frightfulest sight that he ever saw," and inquired what catastrophe could have left them in such a position.

"I thought that they had all started to come right at me," he

added. "I saw them getting up, and their thrones or cat-stools tipping over after them. It did seem so, sure."

The artist has partly verified the statements of the two Charlies, and especially the last.

### SERPENT-CHARMING.

Serpent-charming is a popular diversion in Egypt. One may see serpent-charmers in the squares and gardens of Alexandria and Cairo, and even at the Arab villages at and near the ruins of Thebes.

The serpent in Egypt was an emblem of life and immortality. It was regarded as sacred. Its wisdom gave it a place among the reptiles that were gifted by the gods. Wisdom, disobedient, is cunning; obedient, it is life. Moses may have had this thought in mind when

THE DEALER IN ANTIQUITIES.

he uplifted, as empaled, the brazen serpent in the wilderness, although it is taught that the act represented the conquest of life over the principle of evil. The Israelites had doubtless been accustomed to see the serpent everywhere represented as the emblem of life. In the Boston Art Museum may be seen a picture of a priest uplifting a sacred serpent with his hand, on a very ancient fragment.

At Cairo the exhibitions of the serpent-charmers are well supported by the English residents and visitors. At small places the exhibitors gain a precarious living.

Our tourists met one of these performers at the Arab village at Thebes. His serpents were asps, or the Egyptian cobra. They were about five feet long, and distended their heads when excited.

The Arab seemed to handle them without fear or discomfort. They would move their heads to the sound of music, at his bidding.

"Their fangs have been extracted," said Charlie Noble to Ali Bedair.

The old interpreter repeated Charlie's remark in Arabic to the snake-charmer.

The latter seemed offended. He sent for a live duck. It was brought. He caused the duck to excite the cobra. The latter struck the bird, which soon after died.

Seeing this, the boys took a view of subsequent performances at a long and safe distance.

The boys so often met with the sight of living crocodiles, and had read so much about the sacred crocodiles in their books, that they were desirous of visiting one of the famous caves once sacred to this animal, and still filled with mummies. This could not conveniently be done. But Ali Bedair, on the evening in which the whole party returned to the boat, previous to the day of their return, prepared from an English tourist's account, which had been published, a very interesting statement concerning these caverns and what they contain.

## THE MUMMY CROCODILES.[1]

On sailing up the river, under shadow of the mountain-ranges that on either hand hem in its waters, our dreamy twilight was so often beguiled by natives with wild accounts of crocodiles, and of the crocodile mummy-pits in Upper Egypt, that I was ever on the lookout for the one, and impatient to visit the other.

These mummy pits or caves contain the remains of an immense number of crocodiles, which were regarded as sacred in Upper Egypt in ancient times.

Our party decided to visit the mummy-pits. Passing over the mountains, we came to a scene of wild desolation, and stopped at some rude villages for refreshment, and for further direction to the places of the sacred relics.

In half an hour from the last villages, we reached a slope, central to this desolation, clothed with golden sand, and as smooth and bare, save for stones resembling bomb-shells scattered about, as an arena swept for a festival. In the middle we found the débris of ancient cordage and charred mummies. These were gathered about a triangular-mouthed pit, five feet broad at the base by two yards long at the apex, and ten feet deep, which our guide declared to be the only entrance to the caves.

"And what mean all these charred remnants?" I asked.

"Oh," he replied, "some of the wise men who lately accompanied the pasha in his progress up the country visited the caves, as you are now doing; and on coming out, finding the air sharp and keen, they made a huge bonfire of the once holy mummies of men and beasts to keep life within them, and the rest they threw in fragments away."

At the bottom of this pit was a hole only large enough apparently for a weasel, through which we must torture our way.

Before commencing operations our first inquiry was for lights. Hamed's (our guide's) business always was to provide candles for such expeditions, which it was always Hamed's infirmity to forget. So it happened on this expedition. Instead of an unusual supply for an extraordinary occasion, we had only the remnants of a few farthing rushlights. The question then arose, "Shall we hazard our way with these into the bowels of the earth, or abandon our enterprise?"

Hoping against hope, and enjoining upon improvident Arabs providence

---

[1] Abridged from an English magazine article.

CATS.

and economy, we decided to proceed. Forthwith stripping ourselves of our outward gear, we lowered ourselves into the pit.

It was difficult so to crumple our bodies up as, prostrate and feet foremost, to squeeze ourselves into the weasel aperture. In this posture for twenty feet we struggled our way through a tunnel not more than two feet high and one and a half broad, to reach a grotto, where, to our great relief, we could rise on our knees.

Here we lighted our "brief candles," and set ourselves to the real business of our expedition. This we had no sooner done than our further entrance was disputed by the only living denizens of these gloomy regions.

Clouds of bats, dropping from the roof and walls around, rushed bewildered against us, terrified, in their passage to the open air. Our lights were extinguished in a trice, and ourselves thrown into no small consternation. In vain we battled with the filthy monsters. Swarm followed on swarm, regardless of our cries, and clinging to our bodies with a harpy grip. We threw ourselves down, our faces to the earth, in patient endurance, till the last fluttering wings rallied us from our surprise, and left us masters of the situation and of ourselves.

Relighting our candles, and giving the word "*Dekenkte*" ("Now, then"), to which our guides boldly responded, "*Hadez*" ("All right"), we started afresh, each following his guide, with our Coptic leader in the van.

Resuming our former posture, we writhed again our way through a similar tunnel, to find ourselves in another grotto higher and more spacious than the last. It was a grateful relief to our cramped and bruised bodies; for on account of the narrowness of these passages, and necessary position in forcing our way through them, our heads and faces came into frequent contact with the rugged surface beneath us or the sharp splinters above. Added to this, the increasing temperature of the place, as we advanced, and the atrocious odor of ammonia, made our labor one of such positive suffering that had I been alone I would have made back at once for the outer world.

In this way, sometimes on our breasts, sometimes on all fours, stifled with dust, suffocated with heat, and sick with Stygian odors, we labored on, till in half an hour we emerged into a hall, — if I may so call a chaos of shivered rock, — where we could stand erect.

This chamber, between thirty and forty feet in height, and a hundred perhaps in circumference, which arched over us, and circled round in charred and bristling crags, would, under other circumstances, have imaged to our minds the entrance to the shades; but now, as we sat down to breathe from our struggles, was to us the very paradise of rest.

The rest of a few minutes, however, made us see our position in the true light of the pervading darkness, — a darkness so intense that as we held aloft our feeble lights to survey the scene, it seemed as though it would quench their glimmer.

The heat and effluvia had, at the same time, become so oppressive that I confess I began to fear life and light would go out together. Before reaching this spot, the atmosphere had begun to tell so seriously upon me that I could hear my heart beat, while I was almost fainting from suffocation.

From this hall we penetrated into fantastic grottos and gloomy recesses, to return to the same point, — a bewildering intricacy without end, where, guideless and once astray, you were lost forever. The air, too, had become now so charged with nitrogen that we felt powerless to move, and the tension on mind and body was such as to render us almost reckless.

The Copt at this critical juncture roused us by starting to his feet and urging us onward. His example quickened us to immediate action. Our further progress, however, seemed for some minutes impossible. A fathomless chasm, to judge by our lights, yawned before us. The Copt, however, kept our courage up by continual assurances that he had discovered the tokens by which he had on former occasions shaped his course. Suddenly he descended out of sight, and suddenly we saw him reappear, springing up the further side with a gurgling howl in his throat, which he intended for "Hurrah!"

Directed and encouraged by him, we cleared what seemed an impassable gulf, to find ourselves still prisoners of hope; for, to reach our *ultima Thule*, we had again to throw ourselves upon our breasts and crush our bodies through passages as difficult and tortuous as before.

The rugged face of the rock became now padded soft with layers of crocodile fragments, which the sacrilegious hands of former visitants had strewn on their passage out. The great charnel-house of the crocodile world could not now be distant. One effort more brought us upon several chambers, and at last into one long, narrow cavern, where we had reward for all our toil, as we crawled over the ever-increasing bodies of the crocodile dead.

There they lay, heaps upon heaps, layer piled over layer, from what depth we knew not upwards till flush with the roof. Each layer, where body was separated from body by palm-stems, was thickly and carefully covered with palm-leaves, somewhat faded, indeed, but otherwise as fresh as though plucked but yesterday from groves which formed, as now, the glory of the worshipped river.

The sight, startling in itself, is almost overpowering when you ask, How had all these monster heaps, from the little tadpole of a day to the huge patri-

SNAKE-CHARMING.

arch of three hundred (?) years, been gathered, and in such order, into this pathless world of unbroken night? What spirit of evil ranged them in this cavernous abyss of darkness side by side, the head of one to the tail of another, every chink and interval filled up with reptile-bundles in order due, in strange economy of space? For bundles of little crocodiles, eight or ten inches long, each swathed as carefully as the largest, are disposed in such intervals. Where was the entrance to the shrine devoted to these symbols of the god? On questions such as these reigns Egyptian darkness, deep as that which brooded around us, — a darkness then felt the more, because broken only by the faint glimmer of our expiring light.

My sight grew hazy, and breathing more difficult. The feeble light, which I held aloft, flickered ominously. I felt I must abandon these crocodile catacombs, and I turned my steps hastily toward the upper air.

"Noph shall be waste and desolate, without an inhabitant," cried the Hebrew prophet. "I will destroy the idols, and I will cause the images to cease out of Noph." Thebes is a museum, — a place to buy curiosities. Thebes by day is a long valley of sunshine and birds and flowers; by night she is a stereoscopic picture of desolation. The traveller leans against a column older than Rome, and looks up to the eternal stars, and watches the moon as it rises over the Nile, and thinks the same thoughts and dreams the same dreams that perplexed the minds of men in ages out of mind, and can answer them no more than Job could answer the questions that were asked him by the Eternal and the Invisible.

# CHAPTER VIII.

### A DIGRESSION. EGYPTIAN ANTIQUITIES IN BOSTON.

#### THE WAY COLLECTION.

There are thousands of young people who have antiquarian tastes and to whom antiquities are poems, who can never see the ruins of Memphis or Thebes, or even the British Museum. There is no extensive collection of Egyptian Antiquities in the United States, but there is a small though very valuable one in Boston, at the Museum of Fine Arts. A great number of young people visit Boston occasionally; and we make a digression here to show how a visit to the Museum of Fine Arts on Boylston Street, or Copley Square, may lead to a very instructive illustration of our narrative.

The Catalogue of the Museum says: —

### THE WAY COLLECTION.

The Way Collection of Egyptian Antiquities was formed in Egypt by the late Mr. Robert Hay, of Linplum, Scotland, between the years 1828 and 1833. It was sold after his death, and was presented to the Museum in June, 1872, by Mr. C Granville Way, of Boston.

EGYPTIAN RUIN.

The Way Collection comprises numerous specimens of each division of Egyptian antiquities, illustrative of the arts, manners, and civilization, and of the Pantheon, civil life, and funeral rites of ancient Egypt. Its chief strength is its mummies and coffins, some of which are well preserved; and all would be valuable and important additions to any museum which does not possess similar specimens. Besides these, it is remarkable for its number of small objects, such as scarabæi, amulets, sepulchral figures, canopic vases, stamped cones, and the usual specimens found in Egyptian collections. It is such a collection as the British Museum would gladly have purchased before it was provided with Egyptian antiquities of the smaller kind.

Several fine pieces of sculpture have recently been added, — the gift of the Hon. John Amory Lowell, Miss Lowell, and the heirs of the late Francis C. Lowell. They were collected in 1835 by the late John Lowell, founder of the Lowell Institute. They date from the eighteenth and nineteenth dynasties, between 1700 and 1300 B. C.; and it is to this period, probably, that the finest of the mummy cases and a large portion of the objects in this Museum belong.

It was the period of Egypt's greatest magnificence, though its art had sensibly fallen away from the truth and simplicity that had characterized it in the days of the Pyramid builders (between 4000 and 3000 B. C.). None of the art of that day, excepting, possibly, one piece of stone cut in relief (Case S), is to be found in this collection.

After the conquest of Egypt by Alexander, B. C. 332, Egyptian was to a slight degree influenced by Greek and afterwards by Roman art; an instance is given in the painted mummy-coverings of Case E. Later yet, Christian symbols began to appear, as may be seen upon some of the terra-cotta lamps of Case V.

The mummies in the collection are about three thousand years old. Thebes was then a queen. The glory of Sesostris was her pride. The Nile was a continuous procession of prosperous cities, royal palaces, and stupendous temples.

Moses and Aaron had but recently died. The Israelites had just completed the conquest of Canaan. The rise of Sparta, the overthrow of Tyre, the glory of Rome, and the enthronement of Jerusalem were then events to come.

The Egyptians believed Osiris, the god of eternal life, would be the judge of the dead in the future life. Hence the collections everywhere abound with prayers to Osiris.

The mummies of the collection are six in number, of which four are perfect. They retain their ancient colorings. The face of one is gilded. Upon them are hieroglyphics; there are pictures upon their feet, and on one of the cases is inscribed a prayer to Osiris.

The cases and coverings have all been broken open. Robbing the tombs of Thebes has long been one of the industries of Egypt. Every mummy is searched for its jewels as soon as it is discovered.

They illustrate the curious art of embalming in all of its known details. To accomplish this art the Egyptians removed the viscera and filled the body with bitumen and spices, after which they boiled it and then enveloped it in linen bandages, sometimes a thousand yards in length. The vitals were embalmed in spices, and were deposited in four vases, the first of which contained the stomach; the second, the small intestines; the third, the heart and lungs; and the fourth, the liver.

Certain genii, or minor deities, were supposed to protect these four parts of the viscera; and the cover of each of the four vases bore the image of the deity who was believed to preside over the part that it contained. The vases were sometimes very rich, but were generally made of common stone. They were usually inscribed with hieroglyphics.

The body and the spices having been sealed up, the cartonage was richly painted and gilded, and inscribed with hieroglyphics. The whole was then deposited in two or more wooden coffins, ornamented like the cartonage, and bearing upon its cover, in relief, the image of the mummy, the outer coffin being called the sarcophagus.

In the cases where the cartonage that envelops the body has been badly broken, the form of the mummy may be seen, in this Museum. It seems to have fallen away somewhat from the cartonage. We touched the head of one of these mummies through the cartonage, not certainly with any expectation of gaining information thereby, but from a desire to realize the fact that we had touched the body of a man who lived three thousand years ago.

Figs. 1, 2, 3, 4, represent vases containing the viscera. They are about a foot in height, are very light, and as they are arranged along the shelves, look very stiff and unique.

The covers of these vases, which, with their deep markings and bold features, at once excite the curiosity of the visitor, are images of the heads of the genii of the Amenthe, which, according to Egyptian astrological lore, were a hawk, a dog, a jackal, and a human face.

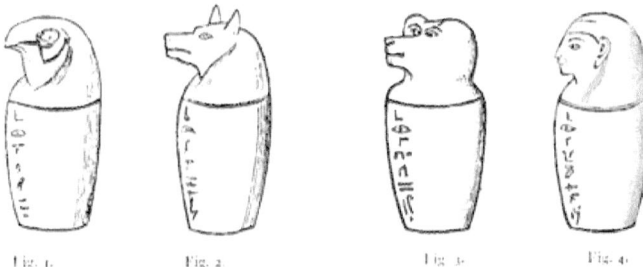

Fig. 1.  Fig. 2.  Fig. 3.  Fig. 4.

Probably the reader will ask, as we did at first, How does it happen that the coffins and images of wood have been so long perfectly preserved?

Egypt, though it is the place where Joseph gathered corn "as the sands of the sea," has a dry atmosphere, and owes her fertility solely to the overflow of the Nile. For this reason wood, if kept dry, will not decay in that country for centuries. It is a somewhat remarkable fact that the fires of a manufactory recently established on the Nile were fed by cedar coffins more than two thousand and perhaps three thousand years old.

These vases and images are, for the most part, such as were known at the time of Moses, and resemble those relics of even greater antiquity, which were deposited in the hills and grottos of Thebes, behind the Memnonium. If they are less ancient, they are counterparts of the relics of the greatest antiquity to be found in the British and European museums.

> "And thou hast walked about — how strange the story ! —
> In Thebes's streets three thousand years ago,
> When the Memnonium was in all its glory,
> And time had not begun to overthrow
> Those temples, palaces, and piles stupendous,
> Of which the very ruins are tremendous."

The Egyptians, when they died, expected to return to their original bodies at some future time, and desired to find them perfect.

Fig. 5

They built their temples with reference to this return, and intended them to outlast the changes of time. They expected to inhabit again the valley of the Nile. Hence the tombs and temples abounded with inscriptions.

But longer records were deposited with the dead. They were written on papyri, a kind of paper made from a plant which has long fulfilled the prophecy recorded of it in Isaiah xix. 7. These records, with the "Ritual for the Dead," also written on papyri, were usually placed inside of a small image, which, like the vases containing the viscera, were deposited with the coffins and sarcophagus. The "Ritual" consisted of prayers to the gods for the guidance of the soul in its gradual elevations into the realms of light, and directions by which it was supposed the deceased would ultimately recover his head, heart, and body.

The Way Collection of Egyptian Antiquities has a number of these interesting images. Fig. 5 represents an image of this kind. It seems to be a female devotee praying to the god of the dead, perhaps for the welfare of some departed soul.

A quantity of papyrus, both inscribed and uninscribed, belongs to this collection of antiquities, and is interesting for its associations. The ark in which Moses was concealed was made of papyrus smeared with bitumen. As Moses was probably educated in Heliopolis, the city of Joseph, and was certainly schooled in all the "arts of the Egyptians," the mysteries contained in the "Ritual of the Dead" must have been known to him, though he has left us only a hint of his own views of immortal existence. The Pyramids were old when he wrote the Ninetieth Psalm; and in its composition he seems to have been more overawed by the shortness of human life and the vanity of its accomplishments than by any glowing conceptions of the destiny of the soul in the world to come: —

"Thou turnest man to destruction; and sayest,
Return, ye children of men.
A thousand years in thy sight
Are but as yesterday when it is past,
And as a watch in the night.
All our days are passed away in thy wrath;
We spend our years as a tale that is told."

In one of the cabinets of the Way Collection may be seen a small image of Osiris holding an Egyptian cross, which resembles a "shepherd's crook," and which was the emblem of eternal life. In another case are small figures representing the eye of Osiris, or the all-seeing eye of God. These were also deposited with the dead. The emblems of the cross and the eye frequently occur in Egyptian inscriptions.

Emblems of the immortality of the soul and of the resurrection of the dead are to be found on all these relics. On one tablet we find a hieroglyphic inscription of the soul leaving the body, represented by a bird or dove flying from the breast of a mummy; on another tablet or image may be seen the soul returning to the body. The beetle, or scarab, was regarded as the emblem of the resurrection, because it deposits its egg in a ball and buries it; hence beetles carved in stone and wood were interred with the dead.

In the collection there is a large glass case nearly filled with sacred scarabs, or beetles. They are made of different metals, and some of them, if we mistake not, are of wood. In symmetry, tracery, and fidelity to nature, they are the perfection of art.

The collection of Egyptian coins is also interesting; for if the more important relics date from 1400 B.C., these may be of much greater antiquity. For aught we can tell, some of them may have been used by the Israelites before the exodus.

But the object that more than any other excites the curiosity of visitors, and to which a poetic mind gives a free fancy, is a delicate female hand, on one of the fingers of which is a small gold ring. It is severed a little below the wrist, and must have been, in its day, very graceful and beautiful. The skin, which is very black, and seems to have gathered a light mould, is drawn somewhat closely over the bones, but not in a manner to give the appearance of a skeleton. The symmetry remains, the ring being still only a little too large for the finger; and it must look now much as it did when the blood coursed through the veins and arteries, bounding with joy or sluggish with grief over events that took place in some narrow vista of the past, no one can tell how many centuries ago.

As the visitor stands by it, he can but wonder what part it had in the drama of life in those effaced years, perhaps before Assyria rose,

Troy fell, or Sparta became a kingdom. Did it strew flowers before the triumphal car of Rameses, or feed the eternal lamps amid the mysterious and shadowy splendors of the temples of the gods? Was it given in marriage? Was it loved and caressed, consigned to a late or an early tomb?

> "Perchance that very hand, now pinioned flat,
> Hath hob-a-nobbed with Pharaoh, glass to glass,
> Or dropped a half-penny in Homer's hat,
> Or doffed thine own to let Queen Dido pass,
> Or held, by Solomon's own invitation,
> A torch at the great temple's dedication."

As we used to gaze upon these mummies and relics of Egypt's storied past and faded glory, the Bible stories that we had learned in boyhood seemed to pass almost like dimly remembered scenes before our mind. In fancy, we saw the selling of Joseph, the sombre grandeur of the court of Pharaoh, the going down to Egypt to buy corn, and the embalming of Joseph, whose body undoubtedly was enveloped in cartonage like that before our eyes.

The scenes of the exodus followed, — the parting of the Red Sea, the destruction of the host of Pharaoh. Egypt, with her colossal monuments, whose fertile bosom once nourished the human race, no longer appeared a vague and shadowy dream. We seemed nearer to Jacob, to Joseph, to Moses and Aaron, than ever before.

We seemed, too, to be in the very presence of the great kings of Egypt; for their busts and effigies are here. In the Catalogue we read an account of the casts. It was as follows: —

"CASTS: The colossal figure is that of Amenophis III., King of Egypt, about 1500 B.C. The original, of granite, is in the British Museum. The placid, benevolent expression is characteristic of Egyptian art. He was the Memnon of the Greeks.

"On the walls are busts of Thothmes III., B.C. about 1600; Rameses II., B.C. 1407; Seti II., B.C. 1300.

"The great bas-relief represents Seti I. (B.C. 1458) attacking the fortress of

Kanana in Palestine. Cast by Dr. Lepsius from the northern wall of the Temple of Karnak. It was under the reign of his successor, Rameses II., that Moses was in Egypt.

"BAS-RELIEF. Nectanebo making an offering, B. C. 378.

"The smaller casts are: Amenemha, a functionary of the twelfth dynasty, about 2800 to 2500 B. C.; Amenophis IV., about 1480 B. C.; Psammetichus II., B. C. 595; Head of Lion, of the date of Amenophis III.

"The Rosetta Stone, inscribed in Hieroglyphic, Enchorial, and Greek characters, was the key to the interpretation of the language of the Egyptians. The original, cut in the reign of Ptolemy V., 205 B. C., is in the British Museum.

"Eight slabs, cast from paper 'squeezes,' taken from sculptures at Thebes. One represents the chair of Queen Hatasu, between 1600 and 1700 B. C."

When you visit Boston spend an hour in Egypt. It will cost you nothing if the day be Saturday.

Our tourists, to gain time, returned to Cairo by a steamer, and thence by rail to Alexandria.

The return voyage had not the novelty of the first experience on the Nile. But the old interpreter made it delightful by his stories. He repeated the stories of the Arabian Nights that are associated with Cairo, and told the original Memphis story of Cinderella. Among his stories that awakened a most intense interest were the two that follow.

## THE OLD PRIEST'S TALE OF ATLANTIS.

The story that I am about to relate to you is very old. The leading incidents were very old in Plato's time. It may have reference to your far-away country, America.

You have pyramids in the New World, I hear, and mummies, and inscriptions on temples like those of Egypt, — in Mexico and Yucatan and Peru: are not those the countries where these pyramids, temples, and inscriptions are found? There once dwelt a race in that part of the world, I am told, who had Egyptian characteristics, but whose history was lost. You should know more about such things than I. But to my story.

FAÇADE IN MEXICO.

Solon, according to Plato, once held a conversation with an ancient Egyptian priest concerning the early history of the world.

This learned priest of Sais related to Solon that nine thousand years before, there lay in the Atlantic Ocean an island or continent "larger than both Asia and Africa." The shores of this continent were near those of the African coast on one side, and stretched an immense distance through the Atlantic, and communicated with mysterious islands and unknown lands. Its inhabitants once invaded Greece and were repelled. This land was called Atlantis, and its heroes were known as the Sea Kings of Atlantis.

In this land there arose at first a powerful dynasty of kings. They conquered Libya as far as Egypt, and were ambitious of the conquest of Europe.

This royal race were sons of gods and of the daughters of the earth-born inhabitants of the ocean land. There were ten kings, who had ten kingdoms, and thus divided the island or continent into ten parts.

Atlas, the oldest son, was the Supreme King. He founded a royal city in the centre of the island, which must have been more glorious and powerful than Thebes. Everything here was colossal and golden; the vast land was a garden; the markets overflowed with delicious fruits.

Atlas had a divine nature. As long as his descendants continued to inherit this divine nature, the glory of their empires was certain to continue; but if any of them were to lose this divine nature, their power was fated to decline.

Centuries and epochs passed. Glorious cities sprang into the air; there was prosperity everywhere.

But at length the kings began to lose the divine character of their ancestors; their human nature began to prevail over the divine. The kings became mere men; their power waned. Then they became monsters; and Atlantis the beautiful sank into degradation, and its people delighted in evil. Cruelty, deceit, and lust prevailed. The gods became their enemies, and forcing the island to sink, the people of Atlantis were drowned by a flood.

Such is the Egyptian story. Other accounts say that Atlantis was sunk by an earthquake, and others that it was driven into the sea by the contact of the head of a comet with this part of the earth.

Diodorus claims that this island was discovered by the Phœnician navigators.

Writers of many centuries have sought to connect this Island of the Outer Sea, or Western Ocean, this Atlantis of the Golden Age, with an ancient knowledge of the New World, through this now submerged course. The western boundaries of this land of godlike kings must have reached what you call the

Antilles: and through such a chain of islands — if the Antilles were then islands — communication with America, especially with southern parts of North America, would have been easy, for Atlantis was famous for its sea kings, as I have said. If the ancient priest's story were true, it might account for the mysteries of Egyptology in your own land, so far away, so far away.

But long after the Fortunate Islands — the Islands of the Blest — were lost, the poets loved to sing of them. Nearly all the Latin poets had dreams of the Golden Age; and Seneca wrote, —

> "Venient annis sæcula seris
> Quibus Oceanus vincula rerum
> Laxet, et ingens pateat tellus,
> Tethysque novos detegat orbes :
> Nec sit terris ultima Thule."

The lines, I am told, inspired Columbus to ask for a fleet for discovery. He sailed over the lost Atlantis, and discovered the lands that once lay beyond it, — the lands from which you come, or those associated with them. And you, my boys, all now think that the Golden Age is in the Western World, so far away, so far away.

It may be that the old Egyptian priest of Sais knew of your own pleasant land, so far away, — a land that the eyes of Ali Bedair can never hope to see, it is all so far away. But Ali Bedair loves to read about that land, and will always remember his American friends when they too shall be far, far away.


## THE BAFFLED KING.

Khampsinitus was one of the most magnificent of the ancient Egyptian monarchs. He was the father of Cheops, who built the Great Pyramid at Memphis for a tomb.

He was richer than any of the kings who had been before him. So vast was his treasure, that he caused a stone house to be built for it, and ordered the mason to construct it in such a way that he (the king) only would know how to enter it.

The commission was too great a temptation for the honesty of the master mason. He fitted a certain stone in the outer wall so that it might be removed by any one who knew the secret.

EGYPTIAN-LIKE RUINS IN MEXICO.

The mason, soon after finishing the royal treasure-house, was stricken down with a mortal sickness. He called his two sons to him, and confided to them the secret of the movable stone.

The king visited his treasure-house often, to see that the seals were secure. One day he discovered that though the seals were secure, a considerable sum of money in one of the vaults was gone.

THE SACKS OF WINE LEAKING.

A few days passed, and he discovered a further loss; and again and again. It was a great mystery to him. How could money be taken from the vaults by human hands while the seals were secure?

He set a man-trap, and so arranged it that if any one entered the vault he would be secured.

At night the two sons of the mason came to rob the vault again, and one of them was caught.

"My brother," said the captive, "I am a prisoner. Cut off my head, or both of us will be ruined. The loss of my head will save you."

The brother did as advised. When the king came to visit the vault, he was astonished to find in it a man without a head.

The king left the body in the vault, but set a guard. The body, in Egypt, was held to be the future home of the soul. Its loss or destruction was regarded as the greatest possible calamity.

"The friends of the thief will try to recover the body," thought the king. "When they come for it, I will arrest them."

When the mother of the dead thief learned the fate of her son, she was in great distress, and said to the other, —

"Secure his body, or I will myself go to the king and reveal the whole mystery. The treasures of Egypt are of less value than the body of my son."

The thief was at his wits' end. He loaded some asses with skins of strong wine, and drove them towards the palace. Just before he reached the treasury-building, he loosened the necks of the skins so that the wine might leak. In this manner he appeared before the sentinels, seeming to be in the greatest distress, running from one leaking wine-skin to another, and calling for help.

The sentinels came to his assistance, but drank so much of the wine in their endeavors to fasten the necks of the skins that they lost their senses, and became dead-drunk. While they were in this condition, the thief secured the body of his brother.

The king was more astonished than ever when he found that the body was gone. He at first knew not what to do.

He issued a proclamation. He had a very beautiful daughter. In the proclamation he gave permission to any man to court her who would answer her first questions; one of her first questions was to be, —

"Do you know who was the thief who robbed the treasury?"

Many suitors came. The thief concluded to go; but he first had made for him a false arm.

When the beautiful princess asked him the leading question, he answered, —
"I do."

"What is the most wicked thing that you ever did?"

"I robbed the royal treasury."

"What the most clever?"

"I secured the dead body of my brother who helped me."

LEAVING HIS ARM BEHIND.

"How?"

"I made the sentinels drunk."

The princess seized him by the arm, and held the arm; but the man vanished. She found in her grasp nothing but an arm.

The king was amazed. He issued another proclamation, offering free pardon to the man who would explain to him all these mysteries. His life and his treasures were all in danger from such a foe. He must make him a friend, and turn his craftiness from ways of evil to some royal good account.

The son of the mason appeared, and explained the secret of the chain of mysteries. Herodotus says that Rhampsinitus gave the princess in marriage to him; which ought not to be true, for he deserved only the punishment of a common thief. But cunning was coin in Egypt in those days, and right and wrong were very little regarded.

## THE MYSTERIOUS ISLAND.

There once lived a man of great riches and resources, who owned a slave, and he desired to make him happy; so he gave him his liberty, and with it a ship loaded with a priceless store of merchandise.

"The sea is before you," he said, "with all its ports and grand bazaars. Give thy sails to the winds, sell the merchandise to the traders of all lands, and all that thou receivest for it shall be thine."

The lateen sails were lifted like wings, and the slave and the ship were borne out of view on the wide and serene expanse of the sea. The mariners were gay; and the slave felt that he was indeed a prince, on his ship filled with costly goods, and flying on over unruffled waters to marts rich in gems and gold.

A storm arose. The ship rocked helplessly, and was drifted hither and thither, like a bubble on the air. She was at last driven upon a rock and broken to pieces, and all the sailors were drowned.

The slave swam to an island that he discovered as the storm abated. It seemed rocky and desolate; and without money or friends, he began to wander about, hoping to find some living being to whom to impart his tale of misfortune.

He travelled away from the coast; and afar, under the dim light of the sky, he discovered the golden domes of a very beautiful city.

Forlorn, and almost destitute of a covering, he journeyed on over the wide plain, a solitary object amid the desolation of land and the treeless expanse of the air.

The people of the city saw him plodding over the plain. A long procession came out to meet him.

"The King! the King!" the people exclaimed. "Hail, hail! The King, the King! Welcome, welcome! The King, the King!"

A golden chariot, with proud steeds and a glittering charioteer, advanced.

The people conducted the slave to the chariot, exclaiming, —

"Joy! joy! Welcome! welcome! The King! the King!"

The chariot and slave, followed by the procession, entered the city, and came to a palace whose splendors exceeded anything in the lands from which the merchant-ship had sailed. Its domes blazed in the sky like the sun and moon and stars.

The slave was conducted up steps of marble, through halls of crystal, into a bedchamber of royal state. Here he was arrayed in royal garments, and saluted as the sovereign of the island empire.

At first he was so dazed that he thought he had beheld a vision, or was dreaming.

He entered the halls of state; they were full of princes and nobles.

"Hail! hail the King!"

"I do not understand this," said the slave. "I am but a wrecked wanderer."

"Hail! hail the King!"

"You do not know who I am. I was born a slave."

"Hail! hail the King!"

"But what is my title to the throne?"

"Sire," said the nobles, "this island is inhabited by the spirits of the air. Each year the sovereign of spirits sends a human being to reign over us. His reign lasts a year."

"And then?" said the slave.

king."

"But is the king happy?"

"He might be if he were wise."

"Three hundred and sixty-five days! one by one they must go and go, each one bringing the king nearer his fate. How could a king be happy in such a state?"

"They drown memory in wine and pleasure," said one, alluding to the kings whom shadowy boatmen had already carried to the mysterious island in the infinity of the sea.

"I will not do as other kings have done," said the slave. "Let me prepare for the future, for the days that shall dawn beyond the three hundred brief days of this one year. There are, I perceive, some wise men among you. Let them be my councillors. I look upon the year of my reign as an opportunity. Let me improve it; a good reign will not end in a destiny of desolation. It cannot do so. It would be contrary to the laws of the Ruler of the universe, whom I serve."

"Naked thou wert sent to us, and naked shalt thou go from us," exclaimed the congregation of the nobles.

"But I will send workmen to the mysterious island to beautify it, and to prepare for my coming."

Then the wise men shouted, —

"Long live the King!"

"I will change the land that looks so barren into fountains and gardens."

"Long live the King!"

"I will make it to bloom like Paradise."

"Long live the King!"

"I will give the sorrowful homes there."

"Long live the King!"

THE MAMELUKE'S LEAP.

"And when my day shall come to give up my throne here, and lay aside my royal garments, *I shall rejoice to go*. I shall only be going to my own."

"Thou hast discovered the secret of life," said the wise men. "O King, live forever!"

The slave did as he had purposed in his heart.

The days passed, one by one, all the three hundred and sixty-five. The

THE SLAVE WAS BORNE AWAY.

slave was daily growing richer in possessions on the mysterious island. His happiness grew day by day, and his last day was the happiest of all.

The boatman came. The slave laid aside his royal robes, and was borne away into the low crimsoned twilight of the sea. The people regretted to have him leave them; but his memory and example, like two angels, remained with them.

The mysterious island at last rose before the slave.

The fragrance of it delighted him before he beheld the shore. He heard golden bells ringing through the mist.

As he drew near he found a great concourse of people waiting to meet him, clothed in beautiful garments. They, too, hailed him as their king. The desolate island became a palm-garden. Golden domes rose above the waving verdure. All the birds of the sea loved the place.

The new king was happy; for his happiness now wholly depended on the well-being of others, and all his subjects were happy.

Then said the king, —

"This is like Paradise."

The winds of the ocean then gently rang all the golden bells, and the people exclaimed, —

"O King, live forever! This is Paradise!"

On returning to Cairo, Ali Bedair made a pilgrimage with his party to the Pyramids; for the former visit to the Great Pyramid had been only an adventure.

## THE MAMELUKES.

Among the places in Cairo that excited the boys' interest was the wall of the citadel from which the Mameluke on his horse leaped. The view of the city and the plain of Memphis from this place was grand and extended.

The Mamelukes were originally slaves of the beys, and were brought from the Caucasus, and at last made their body-guards. In the thirteenth century the Sultan bought twelve thousand of these trained soldiers, and formed them into a body of troops. Their power grew; and they used it for their own advantage, and finally made one of their own number Sultan of Egypt, and founded a dynasty. In 1811 the Mameluke nobles, or beys, were massacred by Mohammed Ali. One escaped from Cairo. His horse, seemingly knowing the danger to which his master was exposed, was made to leap from

DERVISHES

the walls of the citadel, and he reached the ground with his master unharmed.

Ali Bedair, of course, took the party to see the ceremonies of —

## THE DERVISHES.

The Koran commends poverty. Hence sprang into existence different orders of Mohammedan monks, known as dervishes. They are supposed to live in poverty, and to practise self-denial. One of their peculiar religious ceremonies is dancing, and in such a manner as to produce an ecstatic frenzy, which they regard as a very high order of devotion.

Some of the old dervishes do very remarkable things. In their ecstatic devotions they eat scorpions, handle cobras, and pierce their cheeks with long lances. They punish the flesh in many ways, and without seeming injury.

In Cairo the dervishes are particularly numerous. The convents of the brotherhood in Egypt are many, and richly endowed.

One may often hear their night chants at Cairo, as they go to visit the tomb of some saint of their order.

Their devotions do not produce spiritual faces or spiritual beauty of any kind. They are for the most part ill-favored and repulsive. The fruits of their devotions are the opposite of those of Christian faith.

One of their most remarkable ceremonies in Cairo is the riding of a chief dervish on a horse over a road paved with living bodies.

DEFILE IN THE ROAD FROM PALESTINE TO EGYPT

The dervish who is to perform this act prepares himself by prayer, as do the devotees who are to expose their bodies to the feet of the horse. The devotees believe that they will be miraculously kept from

AN EGYPTIAN TOWN.

injury, and that the act secures for them the protection of the Prophet against accident or harm for life.

At Alexandria the party visited the Catacombs, and there were shown "the ends of the earth." These Catacombs were entered by a small hole; and some jackals attempted to come out about the time that the boys were creeping in, — an episode that tended to excite the bumps of caution in both.

"May the Lord have mercy on your souls!" said the guide, as he led the party towards the "ends of the earth."

The inhabitants of "the ends of the earth," like the fabled dwellers upon the earth in primitive times, are able to fly: they are bats.

From Alexandria our tourists went to Port Said, at the head of the Suez Canal, and here took a steamer for Jaffa, the port of Jerusalem.

"I wonder," said Charlie Noble to Ali Bedair, "that the Egyptians never constructed a canal like that, in the times when they were constructing their great works."

"They did," said the interpreter. "This is not the first or the second canal. History gives accounts of two."

"What became of them?"

"They were open for hundreds of years, then became filled with sand."

As our tourists left Cairo, the Pyramids seemed to sink into the sand. The vision of ancient Egypt vanished; for Alexandria belongs to the new civilization of the world.

Ancient Egypt had the ambition of the builders of Babel. She erected her structures to be equal to the greatness of her conception of her gods, and supposed that she was building for all time. Her armies of slaves broke down the mountains and hills, and labored for divinities. Life to them was a passing breath. Their rewards were to be in the luminous regions of Osiris and Isis. They wrought poems in stone for a thousand years.

## THE PYRAMID BUILDERS.

### I.

We hew the quarries of stone, and die, —
    Pharaoh lives, Pharaoh lives;
We rear the tombs to tombless lie,
    But Pharaoh lives forever.
We toil like the scarabs, and then are gone, —
Gone like the lotus that breathed at morn;
    Like the sunbirds we pass,
    And men cry, Alas!
But Pharaoh lives forever.

### II.

We chip the stones of the mountain wall, —
    Pharaoh lives, Pharaoh lives;
We topple the cliffs and cry, as they fall,
    "Pharaoh lives forever!"
From the quarries dark the obelisks rise
With golden records, and face the skies.
    We toil and die,
    And the Nile flows by;
But Pharaoh lives forever.

### III.

From the æons of twilight gods till now —
    Pharaoh lives, Pharaoh lives —
The sun has beaded the builder's brow;
    But Pharaoh lives forever.
Slaves, slaves are we; and our lives we give
That the heroes of Egypt immortal may live.
    We toil and die,
    'Neath the burning sky;
But Pharaoh lives forever.

### IV.

Oh, what are we if Isis may reign, —
    Pharaoh lives, Pharaoh lives, —
And the voice of Memnon is heard on the plain;
    Pharaoh lives forever.
If to gracious Osiris the pylons rise,
And the tombs of the heroes are seen from the skies,
    What though we be slaves,
    And gain but our graves!
Pharaoh lives forever.

V.

We shall live in the heroes who never die, —
    Pharaoh lives, Pharaoh lives;
We shall live in the gods whose fields are the sky, —
    Pharaoh lives forever.
We shall live in the records of deeds divine.
Will the temples of Helios cease to shine?
      We build and die,
      And the Nile flows by;
    But Pharaoh lives forever

VI.

The Sphinx shall face forever the morn, —
    Pharaoh lives, Pharaoh lives, —
And winged peristyles redden at dawn;
    Pharaoh lives forever.
The caryatids forever uphold,
For gods and heroes, the roofs of gold.
      Osiris is just,
      And we are dust;
    But Pharaoh lives forever.

VII.

Oh, give to us each but a bundle of grain, —
    Pharaoh lives, Pharaoh lives, —
One bundle of grain from the blue Nile's plain, —
    Pharaoh lives forever, —
To lay beside us when we lie down
(For the slaves of heroes Osiris shall crown), —
      One bundle of grain
      From the Thebian Plain!
    Pharaoh lives forever.

VIII.

The grain of Amenthi, when goes the breath,
    Pharaoh lives, Pharaoh lives, —
We bear it over the Nile of death;
    Pharaoh lives forever.
Of the grain of Egypt one sheaf we take
Of which the bread of heaven to make,
      One sheaf of our toil
      On Egypt's soil,
    Where Pharaohs live forever

IX.

O Egypt, the nations may rise or fall, —
　Pharaoh lives, Pharaoh lives.
Not in vain to the gods shall thy heroes call, —
　Pharaoh lives forever:
Though Priam's name be heard no more,
Nor Orpheus' song on Ilion's shore,
　　On Thebes's Plain,
　　While the stars remain,
　Shall Pharaoh live forever.


X.

Oh, what is life if to heroes given!
　Pharaoh lives, Pharaoh lives.
And what are toils for the gods of heaven!
　Pharaoh lives forever.
In the heroes and gods, immortal powers,
And earth and sun and stars, are ours.
　　For the gods we die,
　　'Neath the burning sky.
　Pharaoh lives forever!

## CHAPTER IX.

### HISTORY OF ENGLAND IN EGYPT.

THE KHEDIVE. — SUEZ CANAL. — WOLSELEY. — GORDON.

HE land of the Nile is august and venerable in its historic memories. It is the relic of one of those mighty empires which ruled the ancient world. The grandeur of the Ptolemies, the victories of the Rameses, the luxurious splendor of the days of Cleopatra, the greatness of its once flourishing art and literature, are among the most imposing romances of human annals.

Egypt once coped with Imperial Rome in the heyday of its power. It once produced warriors, scholars, statesmen, artists, men of science, who stood eminent among the great men of the earth. Philosophers and students have not yet ceased mourning the loss of that famous library at Alexandria, whose shelves were piled high with the costly lore of remote ages.

In its present condition Egypt is interesting. Its noble monuments of ancient grandeur, its Sphinx and Pyramids, its ruins of Memphis, its towers, hieroglyphics, and obelisks, are gazed at by modern eyes in wonder, and puzzle even modern men of science in the mystery of their construction and the vastness of their scale. The Nile, with its picturesque delta, its rainless borders, its annual overflow, its broad, steady sweep from the strange regions of the Dark Continent, its tropical vegetation, is a rare curiosity among even historic streams.

## THE SULTAN AND THE KHEDIVE.

For many centuries Egypt was a subject province of Turkey. It was ruled over by governors appointed by the Sultan. In 1811, however, Mehemet Ali, who was at that time governor, rose in revolt against the Sultan's authority, and made himself master of Egypt.

Mehemet was thus the founder of the dynasty which now reigns at Cairo. The present Khedive, Tewfik Pasha, is Mehemet's great-grandson. In 1841 the Sultan recognized this new dynasty, and decreed that the Egyptian throne should descend in Mehemet's family according to the law of hereditary succession in Turkey.

Still Egypt did not become wholly independent of the Sultan's rule. It continued to be subject to him in so far as foreign affairs and the army were concerned. The "Viceroy of Egypt," as he was then called, could not send envoys to foreign courts, but was represented at them by the Turkish envoys. Nor could the Viceroy maintain a native army or navy of his own. Egypt was garrisoned and protected by Turkish troops.

Egypt, moreover, was obliged to pay a large annual tribute to the Sultan. Later on, larger liberties were conceded to Egypt by its Turkish Suzerain. In 1866 the title of the Egyptian ruler was, by a firman of the Sultan, changed from "Viceroy" (which meant, simply, the Sultan's representative in Egypt), to "Khedive-el-Misr," usually called "Khedive," which, in the Arabic tongue, means "King."

At the same time Egypt was granted the right to send envoys abroad, and to maintain a native army and navy. But the Sultan still remained the Suzerain (or imperial ruler) of Egypt; and an annual tribute of $1,875,000 a year was paid (and still continues to be paid) into the Sultan's treasury.

This is practically the relation which exists to-day between the Sultan and the Khedive. The Sultan still exercises a kind of exterior control over Egypt, and claims the right to enter Egypt and quell revolt, and to depose or sustain the reigning Khedive.

## THE SUEZ CANAL.

The question has been asked many times since the present complications in Egypt began, What is the interest of Great Britain in the Suez Canal? That interest is both direct and indirect, — direct, because the Government is a large owner of Suez Canal shares; and indirect, because much the largest part of the shipping that passes through the canal flies the British flag.

The canal was first authorized in 1854 by Said Pasha, then Viceroy of Egypt. The concession was made to M. Ferdinand de Lesseps, a Frenchman, — the same projector who is now at the head of the Panama Canal. The company to construct the Suez Canal was organized in 1858. Work was begun soon afterwards, and the canal was finished and opened to commerce late in 1869.

A glance at the map will show to those who do not know it already, that this canal is a part of the shortest route from England to its possessions in India. Out of this fact grew a very strong opposition in England to the construction of the canal. Not that England did not wish for a short line for herself; but there was a fear that if the lines passed through the territory of a foreign power, the water-way might be a dangerous means of attack upon India in time of war, as well as a commercial benefit in time of peace.

But Great Britain had no right to object to the construction of the canal. She merely discouraged the enterprise, and predicted its failure.

But in spite of that, M. de Lesseps persevered, under the encouragement of the Emperor Napoleon and with the direct help of Egypt, and the canal was completed.

The work was accomplished at a vast cost. Although the canal is but one hundred miles long, twenty-five miles of which are through lakes which only needed to be dredged out, the expense of construction was eighty million dollars. Moreover, thousands upon thousands of lives were lost, owing to the unhealthiness of the climate.

Of the whole amount of funds needed to complete the canal, the Egyptian Government furnished about eighteen million dollars. It took for this sum shares in the stock of the company, agreeing, in 1869, that these shares should not be entitled to a dividend until the year 1894. But by the first concession to M. de Lesseps, the Egyptian Government receives fifteen per cent of the tolls.

In spite of the opposition which England had made to the enterprise, her merchants were the first to profit by the new line to Asia. From the very opening of the canal, two thirds of all the tonnage passing through it was British.

But in November, 1875, Mr. Disraeli, then Prime Minister of England, entered into an agreement with Ismail, Khedive of Egypt, to buy all the Suez Canal shares owned by the Egyptian Government. These shares numbered 176,602; and the price paid for them was a very little less than $20,000,000 (£3,976,582), or about $112.50 a share.

## PANORAMA OF THE SUEZ CANAL.

The Suez Canal is, perhaps, the most important artificial watercourse in the world.

We here give a panorama of the canal. It gives a clear view of the whole canal and military field, as will be seen by examining the figures and the following key with explanations.

(1) Port Said is situated at the opening of the canal on the European side. The town sprang into life during the building of the canal. It has a noble harbor, so large that twenty line-of-battle ships can swing at anchor in it.

For some twenty-six miles from the Port the canal passes over the bed of an extinct lake. On the western side lies Lake Menzaleh. (2) At No. 3 is El Kantara; at No. 4, the ruins of Peluse; at No. 5 is Katieh, and No. 6 marks the site of the ancient canal of Necos.

At 7 is El Guisr, the highest point of land on the canal. Here the banks of the water-course are eighty-five feet high. About two miles beyond is Lake Timsah, where the town of Ismailia lies.

This is a canal town, the headquarters of the Canal Company, and only Europeans are allowed a residence there.

No. 9 is Cheik Ennedah, an ancient tomb. No. 10 is an aqueduct. No. 11 is the mouth of an ancient canal, and 12 a salt-water lake. No. 13 is a road; 14, the road from Suez to Cairo; 15, the first encampment of M. de Lesseps, the builder of the canal; 16 and 17, the wells of Suez; and 18, the **reservoirs** of the Nile.

The Attaka Mountains are at 19, and the town of Suez at 20. The harbor of Suez is marked by 21; and the Teel Mountains, stretching towards the southeast and Mount Sinai, by 22.

The isthmus through which the canal passes is ninety-five miles in width, and a careful examination of the plan will reveal an unexpected point of the strength or weakness of the military campaign.

No. 10 is a fresh-water canal, and brings the fresh-water supply from Zagazig, half-way between Cairo and Ismailia. This supply is also conveyed to Suez and to Port Said.

## SIR GARNET WOLSELEY IN EGYPT.

In 1882 Arabi Pasha, an Egyptian minister of war, rose in rebellion against the weak, selfish, and unpopular Khedive; and he carried with him the greater part of the Egyptian army.

Arabi's purpose was to exclude England and all other foreign powers from interference in Egyptian affairs; to dethrone the incompetent Khedive, and to lead Egypt to enter upon a new career.

The decisive victory of the English over Arabi Pasha took place on the 14th of September. Sir Garnet Wolseley, at the head of the flower of the English army, composed of guardsmen, Highlanders and the Royal Irish Brigade, — a force numbering fifteen thousand men, — on that day assailed and quickly vanquished the main body of the Egyptians at Tel-el-Kebir.

This place is between Ismailia, which formed the base of Wolseley's operations, midway on the Suez Canal, and Grand Cairo, the capital of Egypt, situated in the interior.

The English not only routed Arabi's army, but took Arabi himself and his principal officers prisoners, and by a rapid forced march

captured Cairo without resistance, and so practically sealed the
English victory and put an end to the Egyptian war.

Wolseley's exploit was only a brilliant one in its quickness and its
completeness. Arabi's trained force comprised only ten thousand
soldiers. The rest of his army consisted of Bedouin Arabs, fellahs,
irregulars, and stupid peasants, fresh from their fields, undrilled and
undisciplined.

The purpose of England was attained. Egypt lies prostrate at
the feet of the British throne. The English are the masters of her
future. The Egyptian ruler must become the obedient instrument, if
not the satrap, of the victorious power.

A few years ago, the name of Garnet Wolseley was quite
unknown beyond the limits of the British army. To-day he is the
most distinguished living English soldier.

Lord Wolseley mainly served as a staff-officer until he won a
general command. Yet he has been more actively engaged in warlike
enterprises, and has seen more active service, than any living English
soldier. At the age of forty he found himself a major-general; this
being, in the British army, the next grade above a colonel. He had
risen rapidly from one staff appointment to another, from assistant
engineer to adjutant-general; but every promotion was awarded as a
result of his ability and success, and not by reason of wealth or social
influence.

The world first heard of him in the brief, brilliant campaign which
he made seven or eight years ago in Ashantee. There he held the
chief command of the army which so quickly and completely defeated
King Coffee and his sable forces. Wolseley's conduct of that campaign was so signally able that when the revolt of Arabi broke out
in Egypt, he was at once designated as the man of all others to
subdue it.

Leaving England late in August, he declared that he would return
and dine at his club on the 15th of September.

Curiously enough, the battle of Tel-el-Kebir, in which he utterly demolished Arabi, and ended the war, took place on that very day; and although Wolseley did not dine in London, he showed by his playful boast how perfect were his plans, and how exact were his calculations of the time it would take him to put down the revolt.

## THE FALSE PROPHET.

For a very long time a tradition has floated among the Mohammedans of the East that a new prophet would arise in 1882.

This prophet would rekindle the waning faith and the warlike spirit of the followers of Mahomet everywhere. He would free the faithful people of Allah from bondage to other nations, restore to the Caliph (the Sultan) his lost possessions and his decreased power, and would fire the world of Islam with a new crusade. It is thus that the tradition has been repeated from mouth to mouth in the bazaars of Constantinople, among the marts of Damascus, and in the streets and temples of Holy Mecca.

In 1882 an obscure Arab suddenly announced himself as the prophet whom the tradition had foreshadowed. He rapidly gathered to himself a semi-barbarous army, raised the sacred standard of Islam, and began his crusade.

But he was soon denounced in the great temple at Mecca by the Grand Sheriff as an impostor, and was branded as "a false prophet;" and ever since he has been called by that epithet.

Yet he has resolutely reasserted his prophetic power and mission, and marched, with his savage array of troops, into the heart of lower Egypt. He captured the Soudan, the southern province conquered and annexed several years ago by the Egyptian Khedive Ismail.

For a long time El Mahdi did not seem to be formidable. But at last the Khedive sent against him an army of some twelve thousand

SCENE ON THE NILE.

men, commanded by an English officer named Hicks, Pasha. This force encountered El Mahdi at Obeid, only to be defeated, and slain almost to a man.

And then the False Prophet, flushed with victory, occupied the greater part of the Soudan, and threatened the Egyptian fortresses in the valleys of the upper Nile. The Khedive, unaided cannot hope to put down this audacious foe.

### KHARTOUM.

Khartoum is at the junction of two rivers, which used to be called the White Nile and the Blue Nile, from the color of their waters. We now know that the White Nile is *the* Nile, the wondrous stream that rises in the great lakes of Central Africa, flows northward three thousand three hundred and seventy miles, and empties into the Mediterranean Sea; while the Blue Nile is but a tributary, which rises in Abyssinia, flows nine hundred and sixty miles, and pours into the Nile at Khartoum.

What North America was to the world of business and enterprise in 1755, Africa now is; and what Fort Duquesne was to North America, Khartoum is to Africa.

Like Pittsburg, Khartoum is the terminus of one great region and the beginning of a greater. It is the depot of what civilization produces, and the starting-place of the caravans which convey its products to the negro tribes that can give ivory, gold, oil, and cotton in exchange for them. Above all, it is the centre, the stronghold, and the chief mart of the slave-trade, which, profitable as it is, is death to all other trade, and is opposed both to the interests and to the feelings of the English people.

With an English garrison and an English governor at Khartoum, the slave-trade in Africa ceases, and the Dark Continent is practically added to the domain of civilization. If the reader will study a recent map of Africa in the light of the explorations of Baker, Speke, Stanley, and others, he will perceive that Nature has done her part towards the creation of populous and wealthy States in the interior of that great continent.

Khartoum in 1819, like our own Chicago, was a mere military post, established by the forethought of Mehemet Ali. It became speedily the centre of the trade in gum-arabic, ivory, and palm-oil, and its population increased.

For many years Khartoum was one of the most doleful and deadly places on earth. When Sir Samuel and Lady Baker first saw it, in June, 1862, they found it filthy, unhealthy, and utterly repulsive to every human sense.

The point of land at the junction of the two rivers was lined with miserable huts, and the land was so low that these latter were liable to be overflowed. All around, as far as the eye could reach, was nothing but a sandy desert. A swarm of thirty thousand half-naked and dirty people were huddled together in the town, which had neither drains nor cesspools; and if an animal died in the street, the carcass remained to create pestilence.

## GENERAL GORDON.

General Gordon was sent to Khartoum about a year ago, by the English Government, to try and bring safely away from that desert-bound fortress the Egyptian garrison and population. The Egyptians were threatened by the barbaric hordes of the Mahdi, or False Prophet; and as Egypt, by the advice, or rather command, of England had resolved to give up the Soudan, it became necessary to withdraw the Egyptian garrisons from that country.

General Gordon went thither, unattended even by the smallest military force, with only one or two companions, and armed only with a simple walking-stick; he crossed the desert amid hostile Arab tribes holding his life in the hollow of his hand at every stage of his strange journey.

He reached Khartoum in safety, took command of the garrison,

BOATS ON THE NILE

and at once set to work at his task. But before he could find a way to retire from Khartoum with the Egyptian soldiers and people, he found himself hemmed in by the Mahdi's savage forces. He not only could not get the Egyptians out, but he found his own path back to civilization closed upon him.

It is only a wonder how this heroic Christian soldier had been able so long to keep his fierce foe at bay. His force in Khartoum was small, and far from brave or well-disciplined. It was only with great difficulty that he could keep the desert city provided with provisions. Starvation must have many times stared him in the face.

At last it became clear that without the aid of a large force of British troops, Gordon could never get away from Khartoum. Accordingly Lord Wolseley, whose fame had been won by his success on Egyptian battle-grounds, was sent to the Soudan to rescue him, at the head of a well-appointed army.

But Lord Wolseley was too late. As soon as a portion of his force could make its way up the Nile near to Khartoum, it was discovered that the fortress was in the hands of the Mahdi, and that General Gordon, as well as a large part of the Egyptians, had been massacred.

Egypt — which means England — has for the present abandoned the Soudan. Every month makes the condition of Egypt more abject and pitiable. But — in this interpolated chapter — we are getting in advance of the time of our story.

## CHAPTER X.

### THE JOY OF THE WHOLE EARTH

SCENES IN JEWISH HISTORY. — THE "MIRACLE" OF THE HOLY FIRE. — STORIES OF SOLOMON.

"HITHER the tribes go up."

Jerusalem is a mountain city. It is the dwellers upon the mountains who have been great in the thought of the world. The great prophets, great poets, great scientists of the past have nearly all come down from the mountain-tops. The Hebrews were the religious people of the ancient world. Their throne was upon the mountains.

From the Dead Sea to the Jordan the region about Jerusalem is an ascent and descent, — mountain stairs. Jerusalem stands some twenty-five hundred feet above the Mediterranean, and nearly four thousand feet above the Dead Sea. The summits that Jerusalem crowns seem low, because the ascent is even and gradual.

The city was built on two hills, Zion and Moriah. It is surrounded by a massive wall, built by Soliman the Magnificent. The Jerusalem of antiquity lies under ground. The underground chambers, caverns, and catacombs constitute a city grander in its plan and purpose than that which we now see, but over which the earth has drawn her mysterious covering. The tombs of five thousand years are there; the two mountains are the monuments of a dead nation.

The present city covers something less than the space between Oxford Street and Piccadilly in London, and is only about two and a

HILLS AND WALLS OF JERUSALEM.

quarter miles in circumference. It is divided into three principal quarters, — the Mohammedan, the Jewish, and the Christian, — and contains less than twenty thousand inhabitants. Its principal points of interest, beyond its historic associations and antiquities, are the Church of the Holy Sepulchre and the Mosque of Omar.

The Mosque of Omar stands on the site of the ancient temple, on

JERUSALEM.

Mount Moriah. The place is associated, either in history or poetic tradition, with the tomb of Adam, the sacrifice of Abraham, and the throne of Melchisedec. Here the angel of the Lord appeared to David; here David erected an altar; here rose the temples of Solomon, Zerubbabel, and Herod; and here was the palace of Solomon. The ruined fortress of Antonia was here, and the ruins of all now lie at the base of a Mohammedan mosque.

Moriah and Zion were once beautiful, and, crowned with pinnacles and palaces, rose above a region waving with palm groves and green with pastoral valleys. Their beauty is gone. The stones of the ruins that they hide have all been washed with human blood. "Thou turnest man to destruction, and sayest, Return, ye children of men."

In the day of her beauty, prophets and evangelists pictured her in their poems as the type of the celestial city. The siege of Titus caused the death of a million of people; the mountains ran with blood on the day that the Holy of Holies was burned; and the leaders of the triumphant Crusade are said to have ridden through rivers of blood as they planted the cross on the sacred places.

Seven hundred years before Rome was founded the children of Judah fought for Jerusalem. David there contended with the Jebusites. The King of Egypt forced its gates, and carried away the splendid treasures of Solomon. The city was again pillaged in 887 B. C., and the treasures of the temple carried away to the temple of Baal. Siege followed siege; the sixth siege was by the King of Syria, the eighth siege by the King of Babylon. The Assyrians left it a desolation. Fifty years its ruins lay as silent as its stones. Alexander spared the city, at the entreaty of Jaddua, who came out to meet him in robes of hyacinth and gold.

It fell before the Ptolemies. It was taken by Antiochus. It was brought under the rule and influence of Greece. The siege of Herod was the nineteenth, and that of Titus, which resulted in the dispersion of the Jews, the twentieth. Conquered and pillaged by every nation,

the city of Mount Moriah lived on: it fell, always to rise again. The
cities of all her conquerors are dead, — Babylon is a pool, desert winds
sweep over the Persepolis, Thebes is a wilderness of ruins, Carthage
is hardly remembered, — but Jerusalem lives; a remnant of the eternal
nation survives. Could the scattered Hebrews be brought together
from the cities of the world to Jerusalem, the city would be one

THE MOSQUE OF OMAR.

of almost unequalled intelligence, virtue, and wealth; the ancient
structures might rise again, for the Hebrews control the treasuries
of Europe, and have never forgotten the records of the past and the
inspirations of their Prophets, whose moral laws and precepts govern
the whole enlightened world.

The first visit of our tourists was to the place where the temple
had stood, and where now is the Mosque of Omar. The boys read no

INTERIOR OF THE MOSQUE OF OMAR.

books at Jerusalem; they trusted for information to the learning, the imagination, and the willing tongue of Ali Bedair.

The old interpreter talked all the time. The wisdom of the world seemed stored in his brain, and only waiting for ears to feed.

But the purpose of our tourists and that of Ali Bedair in the study of the holy places was quite different. The former wished most to see the places associated with the life of Him whose gospel had said to the world, "Give up yourself and live for the good of others, and God will dwell in your spirit, and make his temple there, and you shall have the ever present evidence of the truth;" who loved others more than himself, and redeemed mankind; whose kingdom was to be a spiritual growth and power, and not vanish like the kingdoms of men.

Old Ali Bedair talked constantly of Solomon; but his companions as constantly felt that once a "greater than Solomon" was here.

"There the temple once lifted its gates of gold," said Ali Bedair; "and there its gates of gold shall be lifted again, some day."

"How large was the temple of Solomon?" asked Wyllys Winn.

"The temple itself was small, but it was plated with gold. It was only about ninety feet long, and thirty wide. But what of that? A little diamond is worth a mountain of glass. When I say that the temple was small, I mean the sanctuary alone. It had a noble court and broad surroundings. It was built after the pattern of the tabernacle, and the tabernacle resembled the plan of an Egyptian temple. It contained thousands of tons of gold and silver; its floor was paved with gold. Its capitals, cornices, and mouldings blossomed with golden lilies; its golden pinnacle rose over the city like a crown, and blazed in the rising and setting sun. But what was all this gold to the Shekinah that shone between the cherubs of the Mercy Seat?"

"Where did Solomon secure his gold?" asked Wyllys.

"From Ophir."

"Yes; but I asked to get your views about Ophir."

THE JEWS' PLACE OF WAILING.

"Sandalwood, apes, peacocks, spices, and ivory are the products of India. The ships of Tyre visited India, and that country was doubtless then in the fulness of her wealth and prosperity.

"Let us now go to the Place of Wailing," said Ali Bedair; and he led them to a court, surrounded on three sides by an ancient wall.

JERUSALEM FROM THE MOUNT OF OLIVES.

It was a desolate place, one of the bare walls rising high above the enclosure; and here was a row of aged Jews, with their faces turned towards the huge blocks of stone. It touched the hearts of the boys to see old Ali join this helpless and hopeless row of men, and lean his head against one of the blocks of stone, and give expression to his grief over the desolation of his country in a deep and despairing lamentation, followed by an ancient prayer.

## THE MIRACLE OF THE HOLY FIRE.

The deception we are about to describe is practised on the Greek Easter. It is a disgrace to the Greek priesthood, and to Christianity in the East. The more intelligent Greek Christians — among them, the priests themselves — know it to be an imposture, and speak of it as such; but the ignorant and superstitious demand the miracle, and were it to be denied them, the Church of the Holy Sepulchre would lose much of its influence over the common people and also one of its revenues. The dramatic event of the Greek Easter is still the Holy Fire.

The Church of the Holy Sepulchre has an air of antiquity, but is hardly imposing. It stands within the modern city, but on a site that was once presumably outside the wall. It is Byzantine in architecture, and stands in an enclosed court in which relics are sold to pilgrims, who flock here on the days of religious festivals, especially on Easter. The Holy Sepulchre stands under the great dome, and is surrounded by golden lamps, and a ceiling of gold, silver, and precious stones. Around the circular hall of the Sepulchre are chapels for all Christian sects. The church is allotted by the Mohammedan Government to all Christian communions.

On entering the church, the visitor is shown the Stone of Unction, which is said to mark the spot where our Lord's body was laid after having been taken from the cross. The supposed associations of Calvary are here.

The holy place is divided into two chapels,— one called the Sepulchre, and the other the Chapel of the Angels. At the entrance to

THE HOLY SEPULCHRE.

the Chapel of the Angels are gigantic wax candles, lighted only on notable days. Here pilgrims take off their shoes, as the place is regarded as sacred.

VIEW IN THE VALLEY OF THE JORDAN.

On either side of the entrance of the Chapel are two apertures, through which the holy fire is given on the Greek Easter. The forty or more lamps in the tomb chamber are kept burning day and night.

Near the entrance to the church is the so-called Tomb of Adam. Here both Adam and Melchisedec are supposed to have been buried. The cross, according to the received tradition in the East, was erected at Adam's tomb. Golgotha was the place of Adam's skull (Matt. xxvii. 33).

Pilgrims from all the Christian countries of the East come to Jerusalem to celebrate Easter in the Church of the Holy Sepulchre, and to see the miracle of the Holy Fire. The crowd within and without the church is so great that companies of Turkish soldiers are required to preserve order.

Our tourists went to the church early, and were assigned places in a gallery. The church filled with pilgrims. All eyes were directed towards the Chapel of the Angels. The crowds were silent, but on every face was a look of excitement. Some were dressed in sheepskin, some were almost naked, some were princely in their attire.

Suddenly a procession began to move around. Then came a procession with banners.

The excitement of the pilgrims became intense. The poor dupes of the long superstition confidently believed that the fire of Heaven was about to come down. But —

The presence of Turks is supposed to prevent the descent of the fire. The visitors were amazed to see the Greek Christians expel the Turkish soldiers from the church. There was a mob, a victory; but no one seemed to be injured. All was but a part of a prearranged and well-acted play.

The Bishop of the Holy Fire now entered the Chapel, and the door was closed behind him. The crowds now surged and pressed upon each other, and the excitement grew. All pictured in their minds the scene in the chapel, and believed that a holy man had gone there to receive from heaven the very fire of God.

A priest stood at the aperture on the outside of the chapel, to receive the fire from the bishop, when it should descend upon the tomb.

There are places in Jerusalem where the selling of tapers for the supposed miracle is a business in Lent. The pilgrims bring with them candles or tapers to be lit by the celestial fire.

A thrilling moment now arrived. Dark arms and tapers were thrust into the air. They looked from the gallery like branches of trees.

There was a flash in the aperture. Every form below quivered with excitement. Celestial beings were in the chapel. The fire of heaven had come. Could a Greek bishop be deceiving the multitude on a day and in a place like this?

The priest received the flame through the aperture. He communicated it to the tapers near him. The flame spread from taper to taper, from hand to hand. One taper became ten; ten, a hundred; a hundred, a thousand. Then thousands upon thousands of lights filled every part of the church. The church was a wall of fire. The air was suffocating. The flames spread, — into the court, into the streets, into the houses. Jerusalem blazed. The city was a sea of fire, kindled, it was believed, by the torch of an angel or the hand of God.

The bishop in the Chapel of Angels, who alone has witnessed the stupendous miracle, faints. Priests bear him out. It ought to make any bishop faint, in reality, to take such a weight of guilt upon his soul.

Our tourists found good quarters, for the East, in the Mediterranean Hotel. After long visits to the holy places, Ali Bedair would entertain them with romantic tales of the Hebrew race. Some of these were quite Arabian in their colorings; for the old interpreter, like all Orientals, loved a royally embellished story. His favorite hero was King Solomon.

COMING TO SEE THE MIRACLE.

## THE WONDERFUL TRAVELS OF KING SOLOMON.

King Solomon had under his command an army of genii, or jinns, — spirits of the air, — who were ready to execute whatever he wished or commanded.

While his palace was building he determined to visit the ancient city of Damascus, and summoned a jinn to carry him thither in his invisible wings. As he was thus journeying through the air, he came to the valley of ants, and was greatly astonished at the sight of the ants' habitations. The ants themselves were as big as wolves, and countless as to number ; and their dwelling-places stretched farther than the eye could see.

He commanded the jinn to stop in the valley, and he there went to the queen of the ants and took her into his arms.

"I am greater than thou," said the queen.

"How ?" asked Solomon, in surprise.

"Thy throne is made of gold and gems, is it not ?" asked the queen.

"It is."

"My throne has become greater."

"How ?"

"Is it not thyself ?"

Solomon was greatly delighted with the wisdom of the compliment, and commanded the jinn to proceed on his way towards Damascus.

Solomon resolved that on his future journeys he would take his servants with him ; and so he ordered the jinns to manufacture a great carpet of silk, so stout that a great retinue of people might be borne on it through the region of the air. The carpet was woven ; but it proved too small for his purpose, and he then ordered the jinns to make for him a carpet on which could be transported a whole caravan.

He wished to visit Medina. The sun was fierce, and to make a shadow he ordered the whole family of birds to fly above the magic carpet in such a way that their wings might make a beautiful feathered canopy.

He dared not trust the jinns out of his sight on these aerial journeys ; so he drank from goblets of crystal, that nothing might come between his eyes and the sight of the jinns.

On his return from Medina he perceived that there was a little aperture in the great canopy of the wings of the birds, through which the sunlight fell on the magnificent carpet, much to the discomfort of the caravan resting upon it.

THE QUEEN OF SHEBA.

"Go, search the sky and the earth, and bring back the peewit," said Solomon. The simple bird was the most useful in the family, just as a little diamond may be of more value than a mountain of glass.

The eagle soared aloft until the earth seemed no larger than a golden bowl. He pierced the transparent air with his clear eye, and at last beheld the peewit amid the rosy atmospheres of the South.

The eagle brought the peewit to Solomon, who had threatened a severe punishment upon it. Solomon arose with a frown.

"I will judge thee," said the king.

"Then be merciful," said the peewit; "for thou shalt thyself be judged."

The peewit trembled, and its wings fell quivering upon the ground.

"How canst thou excuse thyself for thy absence?" asked the king.

"I have discovered a country."

"A country?"

"Yes, Sheba. And a beautiful queen,— Balkis."

"I never heard of her."

"She commands an army that is led by twelve thousand chiefs."

Then Solomon greatly wondered, and commanded that the peewit be protected from harm.

He sat down and wrote a letter to the Queen of Sheba, and gave it to the peewit to carry to her.

The peewit was delighted, and flew like an arrow of light, and delivered the letter to the beautiful queen.

The queen broke the seal, and read it with great surprise. The letter was as follows:—

"Greeting to thee and thine.
"From me, King Solomon.—
"Lord and King over the wild beasts, and the birds of heaven,
"Over the evil spirits and the ghosts of the night, and all kings from the rising to the setting sun.
"Come and greet me.
"If thou wilt come and greet me, I will show thee honor above all the kings who prostrate themselves before me."

The queen sent an embassy to Solomon with a letter.

"If he receives you with arrogance," she said, "do not fear. Pride is an evidence of weakness."

The embassy was very splendid, a procession of gems and gold. Solomon received the letter graciously, and without opening it, told the ambassadors the contents.

The queen had sent to the king a crystal goblet. She had told her ambassadors that if Solomon were indeed a prophet, he would fill it with water that came neither from the earth nor from heaven.

The ambassadors were surprised to hear the king command a negro slave to bridle a young horse, and gallop it about the plain, and then return it to him.

The horse was returned after a time, steaming with perspiration. Then the king filled the chalice with water that came neither from the earth nor from heaven.

The ambassadors returned to the queen, and told her all that they had seen.

"It is indeed true," said the queen. "I must visit this wise and gracious monarch, and do him homage."

## THE QUEEN OF SHEBA'S CURIOUS PRESENT.

The Queen of Sheba, with her twelve thousand generals and all their armies, came to visit Solomon.

Solomon received the queen, sitting upon his throne, in the palace of cedar and gold.

The queen determined to put his wisdom to an immediate test.

Her court was skilled in flower-making. The imitations of flowers were so perfect that the most skilful botanists could not tell the artificial flowers from the real.

The queen brought to the king two wreaths of flowers, exactly alike in appearance, though one was real and the other artificial.

"O king," she said, approaching him demurely but graciously, "I offer thee choice of these two wreaths; which will you have?"

Solomon looked at the beautiful wreaths. His eye could detect no difference between them.

It was a glowing day. Outside of the palace were gardens, and a window looked out upon them.

Solomon knew how to discover the secrets of the vegetable world by the instincts of the beasts, birds, and insects.

Outside of the window he saw some honey-bees spinning through the warm air.

"Open the window," he said to an attendant.

The south wind came into the golden hall of the palace, and with it a part of a swarm of honey-bees. The bees began to alight on one of the wreaths that the queen held in her hand, but they avoided the other.

"O queen, the bees have chosen for me."

Then the queen was made to see that wisdom was the greatest of all worldly endowments, and that Solomon was truly a prophet of wisdom.

THE QUEEN OF SHEBA AND SOLOMON.

The heart of Solomon turned away from the faith of his fathers and the simplicity of the days of the Judges. Egypt glowed in his mind, and one of the most beautiful of all his works was built for his Egyptian queen. With pride came humiliation; with self-seeking, loss.

His works of stone and marble and gold have vanished, but the truth that he taught and wrote remains; for truth is eternal, wherever it is found.

The spiritual life taught in the Scriptures is the treasure of the world, and will always be so; for men will always seek their highest happiness in spiritual things. The invisible kingdom that the Prophets heralded, lives and will increase while the world shall last. But, standing in Jerusalem, superstition clouds the glory of the past.

THE POOLS OF SOLOMON.

One here seems to hear the voice of Him who redeemed mankind, still saying: "Neither shall ye say, Lo here! or Lo there! for the kingdom of God is within you." High above monuments and ruins is enthroned forever the truth that the Messiah spoke to the Samaritan woman at the well.

The visit to the Garden of Gethsemane was made on a Sabbath afternoon, the day following Easter week. A few gnarled olive-trees and a plain enclosure was all; and yet here the travellers felt a strange and tender awe, for here they were brought face to face with a fact that had changed the spiritual history of the world.

Two thousand years ago there came to this spot, or near it, a Being who had come from God. He was deserted. Here he bowed beneath the sorrows of the world, prayed, and went forth to die.

He had preached the gospel of a spiritual life. That fact lives; it multiplies; it is eternal. Egypt is dead; her palaces are dust; her monuments crumble in the blaze of the sun. Thebes and Memphis have vanished from the earth; but the words of Jesus live, — the words of Him whose passion was to redeem the world, re-create the soul in celestial love, and purchase for it an eternal destiny of happiness.

It is the custom of parties visiting Gethsemane to hold devotional exercises. A clergyman often accompanies such visitors. But Ali Bedair at first seemed as indifferent to the scene as the gnarled olive-trees, and almost as silent. He made but a single remark, and there was a volume in the thought.

"You Western people seem happier than we, in the belief that you have a Saviour."

Several of the boys had fine voices.

"Sing," said Mr. Leland.

No one seemed to recall an appropriate hymn.

"I think of two hymns about the Garden," at last said Wyllys Winn. "My poor dead mother used to sing them about her daily work, for we were in poor circumstances then. I would love to sing one of them here. She never thought that I would recall them in this place."

The boys listened with more tenderness of feeling than they had before experienced in their journey. Even the eyes of old Ali Bedair seemed to moisten at last, and all hearts to throb alike in sympathy.

## GETHSEMANE.

While Nature was sinking in stillness to rest,
The last beam of daylight shone dim in the west,
O'er fields by pale moonlight I wandered abroad;
In deep meditation I thought on my God.

While passing a garden, I paused to hear
A voice faint and plaintive from one that was near;
The voice of the suff'rer affected my heart,
While pleading in anguish the poor sinner's part.

I listened a moment, then turned me to see
What man of compassion this stranger might be!
I saw him low kneeling upon the cold ground,
The loveliest being that ever was found.

So deep were his sorrows, so fervent his prayers,
That down o'er his bosom rolled sweat, blood, and tears!
I wept to behold him, I asked him his name;
He answered, "'T is Jesus! from heaven I came!

"I am thy Redeemer! for thee I must die;
The cup is most bitter, but cannot pass by!
Thy sins, like a mountain, are laid upon me;
And all this deep anguish I suffer for thee!"

# CHAPTER XI.

## "EVEN UNTO BETHLEHEM."

### CHURCH OF THE NATIVITY. — RUTH. — THE HEBREW PROPHETS.

ET us now go even unto Bethlehem." They had tarried a week at Jerusalem.

The preparation for the journey had been made on the day previous. All had eagerly anticipated a visit to Bethlehem, and had kept it steadily in view since they entered the Holy Land.

The sun was two hours high when they rode out of the Jaffa gate of Jerusalem. The escort turned southward across the Plain of Rephaim, on the old, long-travelled road leading to Bethlehem. Here they found a delightful country, full of wild-flowers. Bands of pilgrims passed them, returning from a visit to Bethany.

Approaching the solitary convent of Mar Elias, in the hill country, they were soon reminded of the antiquity of the way by coming upon a pure cool well, which the guide informed them was associated in tradition with the journey of the Magi.

"The wise men," said he, "came to this well in their night journey, and here paused, uncertain as to their future course. While in doubt, they stooped over the brink to draw water, and there beheld the Star of Bethlehem mirrored on the still surface below. They looked up, saw it shining overhead, and followed its course to the manger."

The principal object that they met in their journey — an object that was only second in interest to them to the town of Bethlehem

BETHLEHEM.

Hard by this simple but long-enduring sepulchre, Jacob's tents were pitched at the time of Rachel's death. Moses tells us that the sepulchre was standing when the children of Jacob were restored to the land of their ancestry, and Samuel speaks of "Rachel's sepulchre

BETHLEHEM.

in the border of Benjamin." Josephus alludes to it as "over against Ephrath" (Bethlehem). The Jews have recently succeeded in purchasing from the Moslems this shrine of their common mother.

Bethlehem! As they drew near the venerable city, whose history dates back to almost the first records of the human race, the past seemed to start into living reality. Here dwelt Christ's ancestry in the flesh; here in the far past Jacob pitched his pastoral tent, breathed the scented airs of these flowery plains, and gazed upon the stars that shone upon the path of the Magi, and that still set their fadeless diadems in the evening sky.

From this place Naomi went forth to the land of Moab, and returned at the beginning of the barley harvest, bringing Ruth with her.

Time passed on. Jacob sleeps with his fathers. Naomi and Ruth and Obed are gone, and Jesse dwells in Bethlehem. On the neighboring hills David tends his sheep. Here the Spirit of God visits the simple shepherd-boy, and the awe-inspiring prophet comes and anoints him King of Israel.

The kingdom of David rises in power; the temple is built, and the typical glory of Christ is shown. Solomon is here consecrated, and Judaism attains the summit of its worldly grandeur.

Time passes on. In Bethlehem a virgin's Child is born. It lies humbly in a manger, while the glory of God blazes through the midnight gloom. The sky, the hills, the vales, the rocks, of Bethlehem saw these things. They heard the heavenly song, saw the coming of the Magi, and the going forth of the "young child and its mother" into Egypt.

Time passed, and the shadows of Judaism flee away. A greater Light illumines the nations of the world; and Bethlehem, like a monument, sits solitary amid her vine-clad hills.

The town stands upon a limestone ridge, and seemed to display much of its traditional beauty as it rose before them in the sun. But the streets are narrow and dirty, and the houses ill-kept in repair.

One not unpleasant sight at once recalled the former fruitfulness of the country, — the land of vines and flowers, the land once flowing with milk and honey. Rows of beehives were ranged along the flat roofs of the house-tops, evidently well stored with honey from the apricots, plums, pomegranates, and figs, that beyond the town stand blooming or fruiting in the hot sun.

It was market-day, and the old streets were crowded. Here were huge clusters of grapes as fragrant and delicious as those the spies brought from Eshcol. Here were pomegranates, or Syrian apples, which recalled the golden bells that hung upon the hem of the ephod, made in the semblance of the fruit and flower.

Figs in baskets displayed a lusciousness unknown except in the East, and olives and olive-oil recalled the Scriptural figure, "a land of wine and oil." The Moslems, however, do not drink wine; and the juice of the grape, as here used, is not intoxicating.

Bethlehem, though under Moslem rule, is, in itself, a Christian town, thus retaining not only its ancient expression, but its ancient traditions. The first aim of every traveller is to visit the Church of the Nativity, which is the oldest Christian edifice in the world.

The basilica over the Grotto of the Nativity — a place which tradition associates with Christ's birth — was erected by the Empress Helena in 327. It is 120 × 110 feet, and is supported by Corinthian columns of marble, which may have previously belonged to the porches of the temple at Jerusalem. This famous shrine of pilgrims is as ill-kept and neglected as the houses. The pavement is broken, and the mosaics which once adorned its walls have almost disappeared. The church is infested by noisy swarms of dealers in rosaries, crosses, carving on olive-wood, and mother-of-pearl from the Red Sea.

The church belongs to the Greeks, Armenians, and Latins, each of which sects have staircases and passages to the sacred grottos under ground. From the Latin church a rock-hewn staircase passes through long subterranean passages to the tomb of St. Jerome.

RUTH.

An inner door opens, and we enter the chapel of the Nativity, a low-hewn vault in a rock. In the pavement of a small semicircular recess is a marble slab, in which is a silver star, with the words, "Here Jesus Christ was born of the Virgin Mary."

Sixteen silver lamps suspended around the star are constantly kept burning. The whole vault is overlaid with marble and paintings, and studded with gold and silver, and overhung with velvet, silk, and embroidery.

That Christ was born in this place is certain, but there is no certain evidence that this subterranean grotto is the exact place of the nativity.

There is little in the place that appeals strongly to the Christian feeling; it displays Christianity in its corruption rather than in its simplicity and purity. There is something cold and expressionless in all this shadowy pomp, entirely out of keeping with the associations of the humble birth of Jesus of Nazareth.

The sun was descending in a calm sky as our tourists departed from the city. They began to pass through great flocks of sheep and goats, and saw many shepherds. "And there were in the same country shepherds." It was the sight of these, and not the gemmed basilica that they had left, that seemed to vivify the past.

Here Jacob and David kept their flocks, and here the shepherds saw the prophetic star and heard the chorus of the angels. The shadows grew long in the valleys; and in the rosy and golden fringes of the twilight, melted away the sight of Bethlehem.

The thoughts of the travelling company were centred upon the nativity, and the scenes that took place nearly two thousand years ago; all except Ali Bedair's. The story of Ruth and of the family and shepherd days of David rose before him like a vision. It was a kindly thought in the old man, for Ruth was not a Jewess. The great-grandmother of King David, and loved mother in the line of Christ, was one of the first accessions of the Gentiles to the church of the ancient faith.

Ali's introduction to the well-known Scriptural story made the narrative clear.

"The period of the Judges," he said, "was the Golden Age of Israel. It must have been in the old age of Eli that Ruth was born.

"The temple had not yet arisen. There was no king. God cared for his people as a father, and the Judges ruled for God.

"No one has told us that Ruth was fair; yet to every mind she is pictured as beautiful. Why do all the world so picture the face of Ruth?

"Because the true-hearted are always beautiful; the history of a true-hearted man or woman always makes him beautiful.

"Ruth loved the land where her husband was born. She was a true wife. Yet she had no children.

"Ruth loved the mother of her dead husband, — *her* land was the land where the lovely Moabitess desired to live.

"'Entreat me not to leave thee, or to return from following after thee: for whither thou goest, I will go: where thou lodgest, I will lodge: thy people shall be my people, and thy God my God: where thou diest, will I die, and there will I be buried: the Lord do so to me, and more also, if aught but death part thee and me.'

"Blessed Ruth! she had chosen the true God. She followed her mother-in-law, to become a mother of a dynasty of kings. Her true heart had already crowned her a queen."

At the hotel in Jerusalem, Mr. Leland read to all, including the old interpreter, the book of Ruth. The beautiful simplicity of its language, the tenderness of the narrative, and its lesson of the rewards of simple trust and fidelity, all had a charm and distinctness that only the visit to Bethlehem could have given it.

The party spent one day, under old Ali's guidance, in visiting the places associated with Hebrew poets or seers. The first place visited was the Mosque of Omar, whose beautiful dome catches the eye of the traveller from afar. Until the time of the visit of the Prince of Wales,

Christians were not allowed to visit the interior of the mosque; but any one may do so now by paying a sum equal to about five dollars. Here, beneath thousands upon thousands of panes of brilliant-colored glass, was seen the ancient stone altar of King David, the historic threshing-floor of Aranath the Jebusite, the beginning of the three golden temples that were erected above it. The altar stone is about sixty feet by forty. It is a fitting monument of the religious life of David. The angel appeared to him here. It was the place of his religious experience, as Bethel or Luz, of Jacob's.

The place associated with the revival of religious instruction under Ezra, and the pools of Siloam, the traditional place of the meditations of Isaiah, were also visited.

David was the lyric poet of the Hebrews, but the great strain of the Hebrew race was sung by Isaiah. What other poet of all the past ever had an inspirational experience like his? In all the inspirations of the poets, none ever uttered such language as follows: —

> "I saw also the Lord sitting upon a throne,
> High and lifted up.
> And his train filled the temple.
> Above it stood the seraphims:
> Each one had six wings;
> With twain he covered his face,
> And with twain he covered his feet,
> And with twain he did fly.
>
> "And one cried unto another, and said,
> Holy, holy, holy, is the Lord of hosts:
> The whole earth is full of his glory.
>
> "The posts of the door moved
> At the voice of him that cried,
> And the house was filled with smoke.
>
> "Then said I, Woe is me!
> For I am undone; because
> I am a man of unclean lips,
> And I dwell in the midst of a people of unclean lips;
> For mine eyes have seen the King
> The Lord of hosts

" Then flew one of the seraphims unto me,
　Having a live coal in his hand,
　Which he had taken with the tongs
　From off the altar :

" And he laid it upon my mouth, and said,
　Lo, this hath touched thy lips ;
　And thine iniquity is taken away,
　And thy sin purged.

" Also I heard the voice of the Lord, saying,
　Whom shall I send, and who will go for us?
　Then said I,
　Here am I ; send me."

The last visit of the company was to the church on the Mount of Olives, erected on the supposed spot where the Saviour ascended into heaven. Here was shown a stone with a fissure, from which it was claimed that the Saviour left the earth. The site may be that of

THE CASTLE OF DAVID, AND JAFFA GATE.

the Ascension, but the stone is doubtless an imposture. It is not important. It was not sites or holy places, but the descent of the Holy Spirit, that was to be the great fact of the Gospel, and the ground of faith in the Church.

## THE PROPHETS OF JUDAH.

I

DAVID.

The night is still;
The oak of Mamre like a giant stands
In the pale moon. and cool airs come from hills
Mantled with olive gardens and the palm.

         I am
The youngest of my father's sons — David —
And the beloved oft am called.   I was born.
Like Isaac, out of time ; and, as the child
Of his old age, my father's best affections
Cling to me ; and here, near Hebron's sheepcotes,
Where Abraham, Isaac, Jacob, led their flocks.

THE GRAND RANGE OF LEBANON.

I love to tend my sheep, and in the vales,
And on the borders of the clear, deep streams,
And in the noontime shadows of the hills.
To study all the handiwork of God.

God's ways are wonderful!
Out of the nations of the earth he Israel
Chose for his inheritance; and out of Israel's
Tribes he Judah chose; and out of Judah's
Tribe he chose my father's family;
And out of Jesse's sons he chooseth me.

I do remember well the day—
'T was at the new moon of the palmy year—
When to the sacrificial feast at Bethlehem
There came a man with flowing beard and long
White hair; and all the people stood in awe
As he approached the altar. In his hand
He bore a horn of holy oil, and beside him
Led a heifer white as his own hair.

I was among the flocks
When, lo! there came a messenger to me,
And I was called to join my father's family.
I lifted up my face in joy to God,
Then left the white flocks in the valleys.

The aged man
Hailed me with gladness, bowed his head, and said,
"The Lord has chosen *him*;" and then he poured
Upon my head the holy oil, and then
The heifer sacrificed, and, after, turned
Away mysteriously as he had come.

I returned
To Hebron's sheepcotes, tuned my harp and sung,
Out of the mouths of babes hath God perfected
Praise. My head with oil he doth anoint,
My cup with joy runs over!

'T is full-orbed night.
The flocks that I have safely led all day
To the refreshing pastures, cleft by streams,
Now safely slumber; not one of them is lost.

The wind breathes through my harp
As though an angel touched it,—my harp
That I have carried long to cheer my thoughts
Among these silent hills and lonesome valleys
Of the shade of death. An inspiration
In me wakes: ofttimes at night God gives
Me songs, and I will touch again the sweet
Low chords:

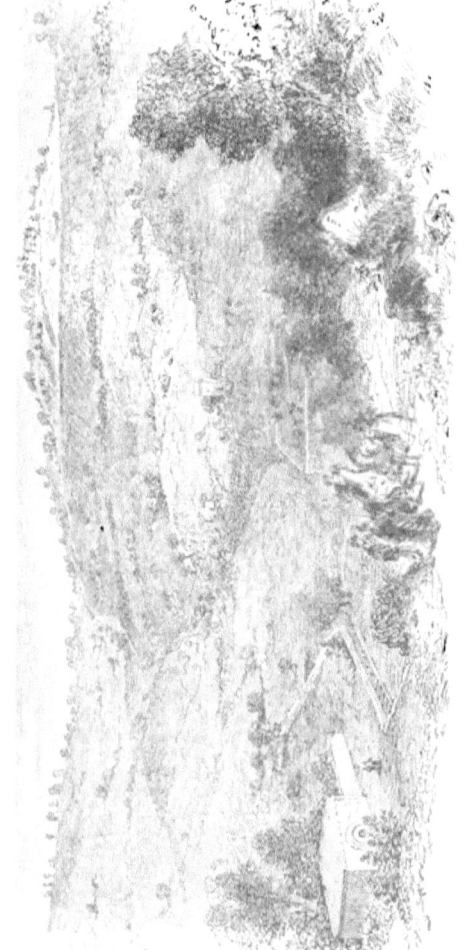

MOUNT OF OLIVES.

## "EVEN UNTO BETHLEHEM."

I.

How beauteous is the night!
Alleluia!
The heavens declare the glory of the Lord,
The firmament displays his glorious word
In characters of light.
Awake, my harp, awake!
Alleluia!

II.

On such a night as this,
Alleluia!
The Shiloh shall descend from heaven's throne;
The hosts cherubic the descent shall own
In harmonies of bliss.
Awake, my harp, awake!
Alleluia!

III.

The latter days I see.
Alleluia!
Fairer than earthly sons, with lips of grace
He comes, with mercy beaming in his face,
To set sin's captives free.
Awake, my harp, awake!
Alleluia!

IV.

Lift up your heads, ye gates!
Alleluia!
And be ye lifted up, ye everlasting doors!
To God earth's kingdom the Messiah restores
That his salvation waits.
Awake, my harp, awake!
Alleluia!

V.

Glory to God on high!
Alleluia!
Yon star seems glowing over Bethlehem;
In all night's coronet the brightest gem,
The fairest in the sky.
Awake, my harp, awake!
Alleluia!

VI.

I see what seers have seen,
    Alleluia!
And all my soul with holy rapture thrills;
The dayspring breaks upon the dewy hills
    And on the pastures green.
        One sweet chord more awake!
            Alleluia!


II.

EZRA.

When Israel's tribes, from Babylonia, pressing
    Towards Zion, raised their psalms,
And once again their native vales possessing,
    Bowed 'neath the pastoral palms,

GROTTO OF THE NATIVITY, BETHLEHEM.

And saw the hills with purple vineyards growing
    Above the Jordan fair, —
They called to mind the fiery pillar, glowing
    Amid the desert air.

The ransomed chiefs recalled with joy, discerning
    The Hand that made them free,
The far-off domes of Babylonia burning
    Above the white sand sea.

VALE AND CITY OF NAZARETH.

They built their altar, and with memories tender
    Their peaceful homes begun,
And rose the city in its ancient splendor
    Beneath the Syrian sun.

New walls they built, the holy shrine defending,
    New streets the prophets trod;
Then Ezra spake, the prophet's hill ascending,
    "Hear ye the Word of God!"

Then reverent feet the sacred hill surrounded,
    The chief, the sire, the youth:
"O Israel, hear! The nation ye have founded
    Must know God's Word of truth."

The ancient law, first to the rabbi given,
    Fell from the prophet's tongue;
And 'neath the blue pavilion of the heaven
    The choirs of Asaph sung.

The old and young beneath the palms were seated,
    Where the deep fountains lay.
The Rabbi lessons from the Law repeated, —
    'T was Judah's Bible-day.

They brought from mountains, from the brooks and meadows,
    The myrtle, palm, and pine;
And made them tents, and in the fragrant shadows
    Rehearsed the Word Divine.

There they recalled the seraph-crowned mountain,
    When God to Sinai came,
And told the tales of Meribah's sweet fountain,
    And pillared cloud and flame.

Green grew the white streets of the city beauteous,
    Each place of palms and pools;
And in those green tents, filled with households duteous,
    Were Ezra's Bible-schools.

O glorious days! — days of the open vision
    And answers swift to prayer,
When walked the priest so near the realms elysian,
    He breathed immortal air.

O'er Shusan's palace drift the sands relentless,
    And herbless lie and deep,
On that dead plain, where Babylonia tentless
    Sleeps her immortal sleep.

Persepolis is dead, and Judah lonely
    Sits with discrownèd brow ;
Of all those scenes, the Bible lessons only
    Live with the nations now.

## CHAPTER XII.

### THE SULTAN AND PALESTINE

THE SULTAN. — PALESTINE. — A FAMILY THAT COULD NOT BE CONQUERED.

THE young mind naturally asks how it is that the historic Hebrew race, the moral law-givers of the world, should be so largely under the dominion of the Mohammedan Sultan, and that Palestine should be a dependency of the weakest of the European powers.

The Ottoman Empire, with its provinces, corresponds in many respects to the old Byzantine Empire in the period of her splendor and progress. It arose on the ruins of that old empire, and the faith of the False Prophet became the inspiration of its arts and arms. Mohammed II. (1451–1481), called the Conqueror, was the founder of the greatness of Turkey. He conquered Constantinople in 1453. Among his ambitious successors was Selim I. (1512–1520), who conquered Mesopotamia, Syria, and Egypt. His son Soliman the Magnificent completed the conquest of the Levant. In the sixteenth century Turkey reached the height of her power.

Turkey in Europe numbers nearly nine million inhabitants, and Turkey in Asia a little more than thirteen million. Of these one hundred and fifty thousand are Jews.

The Crusades, as has been explained in another volume, were organized to liberate Palestine from the rule of the Sultans, and to secure the Holy Places to the Christian world. They failed. For hundreds of years the Turkish Empire has seemed tottering to its fall; but though weakened, its old boundaries and dependencies continue, and Constantinople is the throne of the East.

## THE SULTAN.

Abdul Hamid, the present Sultan of Turkey, is a brother of the unfortunate Murad, who preceded him, and was deposed, and is a younger son of the Sultan Abdul Medjid. His advent to the Turkish throne was sudden; for Murad, after a very brief reign, became insane, and thus was unfitted to govern. At the time of his accession the world knew almost absolutely nothing of young Abdul Hamid.

Less than thirty years of age, with but a remote prospect of ever ascending the throne, he had always led the obscure and retired life to which all Turkish princes of the blood are subjected. Of a sudden he appeared on the pinnacle of power, and that at a moment when, above all things, experience and statesmanship seemed to be needed to save the Turkish Empire in Europe from destruction.

It soon appeared that Hamid was an abler and more energetic man than his brother. He devoted himself with zeal to his most difficult duties; he proved free from many of the debasing vices which have disgraced the lives of so many sultans; and he showed too much sense to cling obstinately to despotic power at a time when wisdom lay in concession and conciliation. The Sultan Abdul Hamid is described as rather tall and slight in form, with an oval and swarthy face, large dark eyes, and short black hair, while he wears a long, sweeping, black mustache, and no other beard.

In manner he is quiet, serious, and dignified. His habits are good. He rises early, and devotes many hours a day to councils of his ministers and the business of the State. He is accomplished in several languages; and the forced retirement of his life before he ascended the throne was spent in study and reading rather than in the indolent pleasures of the Ottoman court.

It would be a great mistake to suppose that Turkey, however bad her government has become, is wanting in able and enlightened statesmen. There has seldom been a period when the councils of the Sultan have not contained men of eminent talents and broad views. The late Fuad Pasha, who declared that Turkey must follow the lead of the other European nations in liberty and progress, was the equal, perhaps, of any statesman on that Continent.

His first Grand Vizier was Midhut Pasha, a statesman of liberal views. Under his influence the young Sultan granted to Turkey a constitution which guaranteed a legislature composed of a Senate to be nominated by him, and a Chamber of Deputies to represent the people. In this assembly the provinces, for the first time for centuries, had a voice.

The first meeting of the Turkish Parliament took place in March, 1877, in the palace at Constantinople.

The ceremony of opening the Parliament was a brilliant and imposing one. The palace of Dolma-Baghtche stands upon the shore of the sparkling Bosphorus, and rises, with its white marble walls and columns, amid a forest of domes, pavilions, and minarets. It has a great hall, which is spacious and lofty, and fairly dazzles the eye with its decorations of gold.

The approaches to the palace were crowded at an early hour by a multitude, among whom appeared the many fantastic and brightly colored costumes of the East. The hall itself was lined with the Sultan's guards, in scarlet coats and high crimson velvet hats, in shape resembling helmets, with large plumes.

When the hour of the ceremony was near, the hall gradually filled with the great dignitaries of Church and State, each wearing a gorgeous costume peculiar to his office, and the stars of the various Turkish orders of knighthood.

At one end of the room was a gorgeous throne, which was said to be of pure gold; at least, so it looked, being entirely of a glistening golden hue. When all the great people had taken their places, the Grand Vizier entered; and then, surrounded by his chief courtiers, appeared the pale face of the young Sultan Abdul Hamid.

The Sultan was much more plainly dressed than many of the personages around him. He wore an unadorned blue coat and simple red fez, and at his side swung his State sword. He advanced slowly to the throne, while the dignitaries on either side bowed almost to the earth; when he reached it, he looked around quietly and bowed slightly.

Then he motioned to the Grand Vizier, who came forward, bowing at each step so low that his right hand touched the floor. The Sultan handed him a roll of paper, which the Grand Vizier kissed, and gave over to the Sultan's secretary. This official unrolled it, and amid profound silence read its contents. It was the Sultan's speech, opening his first Parliament. This over, the Sultan proceeded out of the hall; as he emerged from the palace, salvos of artillery boomed over the Bosphorus; and the ceremony was at an end.

It was the first gleam of Turkish political liberty in the Levant.

## TURKISH PALESTINE.

The word Palestine is synonymous with Philistia, and was given to the southern portion of the Jewish kingdom. The Romans, after the conquest of the Jews, gave the name to the whole province, or kingdom. The ancient harbor of Cæsarea was the principal port of Palestine during the Roman dominion.

The country was subject to the Roman and Byzantine emperors for some six hundred years of the early Christian era. After the destruction of Jerusalem by Titus, the Jews became exiles and slaves, and were driven into nearly all parts of the world.

Christianity spread. The Holy Places of Jerusalem became shrines for the pilgrims of all Christian lands. Helena and Constantine erected chapels and altars there, and monumented the places of sacred scenes and associations. The land was conquered by the Persians, the Arabs, the Egyptians, and the Turks. Then came the romantic period of the Crusades, during the rule of the Egyptian sultans. The sultans of Egypt held the country until 1517, when it was conquered by the Turks; and it has remained a Turkish province until the present time, with the exception of a brief occupation by Egypt. As the government of the Sultan becomes more liberal, the Turkish restrictions in Palestine are made less severe.

Titus broke the Jewish power. The Hebrew nation has never been strong or united since the temple fell, in the first century of the Christian era.

The Jews gave their blood like water for their city and temple.

Old Ali Bedair loved to relate tales of that heroic epoch, and to contrast the spirit of that final struggle with the patriotic records of other lands.

One of his stories of the heroism of his ancient ancestors left a vivid picture in the mind.

## A FAMILY THAT COULD NOT BE CONQUERED.

The city fell; the temple departed in fire: but the old spirit lived in the families of the dead heroes.

There was a widow in Jerusalem who had seven sons. Her husband had died in the siege.

"Bring the family before me," said the conqueror, who had learned that they were of noble birth and true to the faith of the patriarchs.

They were brought into the palace.

"Thou must pay homage to the gods of Rome," he said to the eldest son.

"Our law says, 'I am the Lord thy God.' To no other god will I bow."

"Let him be taken to execution," said the conqueror.

"Thou must worship the gods of Rome," he said to the second son.

"My brother did not; neither will I."

"Wherefore?"

"The second law says, 'Thou shalt have no other gods but me.'"

"Let him follow his brother to death."

"Wilt thou worship the gods of thy conquerors?" he said to the third.

"Never!"

"Wherefore?"

"I bow to the fate of my brothers, and honor their example; but never will I worship what is false."

"Let him share the fate of his brothers," said the conqueror.

"Wilt thou worship my gods?" he demanded of the fourth.

"Never!"

"Wherefore?"

"God is God."

"Let him die."

"Art thou like the others?" he asked of the fifth.

"'God is one. Hear, O Israel!'"

"Lead him away."

"Obstinate, like the rest?" he asked of the sixth.

"God is terrible."

"Go."

"My son, thou art young and fair," he said to the seventh. "Keep thy life. Thou art but a child."

"'The Lord, he is God, in the heavens above, and in the earth beneath.'"

"So young, so fair. Bow, and the future is thine."

"The Lord shall reign forever."

"I will drop my ring for the sake of the gods. Pick it up, my child, and thou shalt be spared."

"Let it lay where it fell. I fear life without God, but I fear not man."

"If thy God be great and merciful, why does he not deliver thee, as thou sayest he delivered thy fathers of old?"

"I am not worthy of redemption, neither art thou worthy to witness a display of God's power."

"Thou shalt join thy brothers."

"And, woman, what sayest thou?" he demanded of the widow.

"Abraham built one altar for the sacrifice of his son; I have built seven, and made the offerings. Let me join my sons."

## CHAPTER XIII.

### ATHENS

ATHENS. — IN THE STREETS OF ATHENS. — HOW PEOPLE TRAVEL IN GREECE.

OPPA the beautiful, the father of the ports of the world, looks like a ruined temple from the sea, like one colossal building. To the port of Joppa the cedars of Lebanon were sent "in flotes" for the building of the temple.

The gardens around the city are lovely; but the beauty of Joppa disappears when the city is entered, whether it be from the land or from the sea.

Charlie Noble and Wyllys Winn were invited by Frank Gray to go with him to Athens, and there visit the American School of Classical Studies, and the scenes and associations of Greek literature and art. They accepted the invitation.

It had been Frank Gray's purpose to induce the whole party to return with him to Athens; but Mr. Leland decided to rest awhile at Joppa and Jerusalem, and then, in company with Charlie and Ali Bedair, to go to Damascus and the ruins of Palmyra, or to Persia and India, as his health should determine. Ali Bedair and Charlie at the last moment also accepted Frank Gray's invitation, and accompanied him and his companions to Greece.

The party divided at Joppa.

Frank Gray and his friends waited here two days for the steamer to the Piræus. They spent the time in visiting the bazaars and the so-called house of Simon the Tanner, now a kind of mosque.

Joppa, in old story, is made the place where Noah entered the ark. It has a long and splendid history during the Christian era of the struggles of the West for Palestine. At present the best thing about the city would seem to be its oranges, which are the finest, or among the finest, in the world.

The harbor is shallow. The boys reached the steamer by boats. The steamers to the port usually lie in the roadstead, a half-mile distant from the quay.

"How much will your trip cost you?" asked Mr. Leland of Charlie Noble, as they were about to part.

"Less than five hundred dollars, I hope," said Charlie. "It would have cost me much more; but I went as your guest from Cairo to Thebes, and I go on Frank Gray's invitation to Athens. But I find that my visit to Alexandria, Cairo, the ruins of Memphis, Jerusalem, and Bethlehem, including return fare to New York, will cost me about five hundred dollars. A person whose passion for travel would lead him to be very economical could visit the three great cities of history, Alexandria, Cairo, and Jerusalem, including *Bethlehem*, for that sum."

The low figures for fares of the World Travel Co., New York (1885), are as follows: —

ROUTE 132.

New York, Liverpool, Glasgow or London, Dover or Folkestone, Paris, Turin, Genoa, Rubattino steamer to Alexandria, Cairo, steamer to Naples, rail to Rome, Florence, Venice, Milan, St. Gothard, Lucerne, Bâle, Paris, Calais or Boulogne, London, Liverpool or Glasgow, New York.

This tour can be accomplished in sixty days, exclusive of ocean travel.

|  | 1st Cl. | 2d Cl. |
|---|---|---|
| Anchor, Cunard, Guion, Inman, White Star Lines to Liverpool | $415.35 | $381.50 |
| Allan Line to Liverpool | 385.35 | 351.50 |
| National Line to Liverpool | 355.35 | 321.50 |
| Anchor Line to Glasgow | 389.35 | 352.84 |
| State Line to Glasgow | 379.35 | 342.84 |
| National and Monarch Lines to London | 331.35 | 300.84 |

SIDE TOURS IN EGYPT AND THE HOLY LAND.

|  | 1st Cl. | 2d Cl. |
|---|---|---|
| *a.* Alexandria to Cairo and back | $11.96 | $7.96 |
| *b.* Alexandria to Cairo, Ismailia, Suez Canal, Port Said | 14.33 | 11.10 |

THE SUBURBS OF ATHENS.

*c.* Jaffa to Jerusalem and back; horse, or seat in a carriage . . $19.60
*d.* Short tour, occupying three days, from Jerusalem to Bethlehem, Solomon's Pool, Mar Saba, Dead Sea, Jordan, Jericho, back to Jerusalem . . . . . . . . . . . . . . . 22.50

ROUTE 133.

New York, Liverpool, Glasgow or London, New Haven, Dieppe (or via Dover and Folkestone at increased fares), Paris, Turin, Venice, Trieste, Austrian Lloyd steamer to Alexandria, Cairo, Ismailia, Port Said, Jaffa (for Jerusalem and inland Palestine tour). Beyrout (for Damascus and Baalbec), Alexandria, Brindisi, Naples, Rome, Florence, Venice, Milan, Turin, Paris, Rouen, London, Liverpool or Glasgow, New York.

This tour can be accomplished in seventy days, exclusive of ocean travel.

|  | 1st Cl. | 2d Cl. |
|---|---|---|
| Anchor, Cunard, Guion, Inman, White Star Lines to Liverpool | $465.85 | $429.60 |
| Allan Line to Liverpool | 435.85 | 399.60 |
| National Line to Liverpool | 405.85 | 369.60 |
| Anchor Line to Glasgow | 439.85 | 400.94 |
| State Line to Glasgow | 429.85 | 390.94 |
| National and Monarch Lines to London | 381.85 | 348.94 |

Members of the School met the boys at the Piræus, — the port of Athens. We have given a view of the ancient temples of the city in another volume, and shall speak chiefly of social life and travel here.

It is one of the remarkable changes of civilization that American youth should have the opportunity of finishing their classical studies here, amid the very scenes and associations of the literature they are pursuing. The time is soon coming when American scholars preparing to teach the classics will at least wish to complete their studies in Athens, should the American School there prove successful.

IN THE STREETS OF ATHENS.

The story is told of old Ulysses, that after an absence of twenty years from his home, he was borne by the Phæacians across the seas, and placed while asleep on the shore of his native island. In order that we may take a view of what our friends saw, let us try to believe that we, either by the Phæacians or by means of some magic carpet, have been transported across the seas in the night, and have waked up in the old city of Athens.

It is a strange cry that breaks our slumbers. "Gala! gala!" says the voice; and we rush to the window to see what sight awaits us, when, to our disappointment, we behold a modern milk-cart, and conclude that "gala" must be the Greek word for milk, and this must be the milkman's cry.

Scarcely have we made this new discovery before the words "Selapi zesto! Selapi zesto!" fall on our ear, and we wonder what this "Selapi zesto," which some one is carrying about in a tin pail, can be. We find on inquiry that it is a warm drink made of something like arrowroot, and that the Greeks are very fond of it, and often take it before rising in the morning.

As we sit at our breakfast of coffee, rolls, and wild honey from Mount Hymettus, the sound of fife and drum arouses our curiosity, and we learn that the royal guard is being changed.

It is thought to be necessary everywhere to guard kings and queens, you know; and so a certain number of soldiers stand about the palace for a certain length of time, and then are relieved by others.

After breakfast we start out on an exploring expedition through the streets of this interesting old city.

The sun shines out warm and bright; the soft air floats in from the sea.

As we walk along the well-paved streets, and look at the fine stone and marble houses in the new part of the city, we forget also that we are out of New York or Boston, until a donkey, laden with panniers of fruits or vegetables, or covered all over with brushwood, appears upon the scene, and then we wake up to the fact that this is a country where the traffic is carried on by donkey-lines instead of express-lines. The donkeys and their drivers stop in front of the doors, and the housewives supply themselves for the day; or perhaps the donkeys do not deposit their burdens till they reach the general market.

PORT OF PIRÆUS.

Let us take a walk first in Hermes Street, which is one of the principal business thoroughfares of the city, and on our way we will pass the king's palace.

It is a great, square, brown stuccoed building, so very bare and ugly that we are sure that you would never be tempted to become King or Queen of Greece for the sake of living there. There is nothing to be seen save the dusty plot in front, and the few soldiers on guard; so we pass through a small park, and find ourselves at the opening of Hermes Street, the Broadway of Athens.

It was very appropriate to name this street after the old god Hermes, for he was the patron of merchants, and here is where the merchants have a large part of their finest stores.

Many of them look like those we see in America. Here are dry-goods stores and millinery establishments and jewelry shops, where perhaps the windows glitter with diamonds; for diamonds are cheaper in Athens than in America. Here are shops for books and pictures, for glass and china. The china tempts us, and we go in to look at the delicate little cups for after-dinner Turkish coffee, — cups decorated with Athena's head, and the Greek border in blue and gold.

Next door is a Turkish shop, a little room not larger than a common clothes-closet. Here the Turk sits cross-legged on his counter, and hands down from the well-filled shelves any number of tempting Turkish and Persian rugs, beautifully embroidered table-spreads, fezes, costumes, pipes, and, in fact, almost everything that one finds in Constantinople itself.

As we pass on, we see in a window what seems to be a dead animal, lying on his back with feet in the air. We stop, and ascertain that it is the skin of an animal filled with lard; and as the lard is cut off for customers, the skin is opened and turned back. It makes one think of the goat-skins for carrying water and wine, used in the time of Christ, and even now in the East. Outside of this shop stand casks of wine and olive-oil, waiting for customers.

Most of the people dress as we do; but it is very easy to select many who are attired in peculiar and picturesque costumes.

Here is the peasant from the neighboring country, with his scarlet fez and dark blue cotton jacket and trousers. The fashion of his trousers never changes, for they are always made like a great square bag, gathered at the waist, and with holes in the two lower corners for the feet to pass through.

Here is the elderly man of Athens, who clings to the national costume; and well he may, for he will tell you that he fought in the Greek Revolution. He makes a pretty picture, attired in scarlet fez, with blue or black tassel, a short scarlet mantle hanging loosely from his shoulders, beautifully embroidered jacket, a white kilt skirt coming to the knees, handsome leggings braided with scarlet and gilt, and prettily ornamented Greek shoes.

This picturesque old gentleman attracts us all the more if he happens to walk by the side of a Greek priest who dresses in a straight black gown, coming to the feet, and wears on his head something that looks exactly like a piece of stove-pipe a foot high, covered with black cloth.

During the Carnival days one meets long lines of carriages, filled with people wearing masks and dressed in every imaginable fashion. There are also trains of donkeys, whose riders are so disguised as to render them more like donkeys than men.

One character at the Carnival, we were told, was a little boy, who actually hid himself inside of a goat's skin, head and all; and so looked like a veritable goat, walking on his hind feet, with a belt of bells about his waist. He was trying to make himself into a Satyr of the olden time.

In contrast with such a scene one may hear the low, monotonous dirge of the priests, and, aware that a funeral procession is coming, step one side to see this peculiar spectacle. There is no long line of carriages, as with us; but every one walks.

THE ATHENIAN CARNIVAL.

First come the priests in white robes, chanting a funeral dirge. Then follows a man bearing upright the coffin-lid, which is white and ornamented with a large cross and artificial flowers. After this walk the bearers with the open coffin, thus exposing the deceased to the gaze of every one. Lastly come the friends and the curious crowd, who always follow.

A hearse or catafalque is sometimes used, but the body is not often put into it until after the city limits are passed.

If we go out to the cemetery, we find that on the new-made graves earthen jars have been broken, as a symbol that "the silver cord is loosed, the golden bowl is broken."

And now, after having wandered somewhat up and down the streets of Athens till we are too weary to enjoy more, we start for home.

We step into the market a moment, to take a hungry look at the oranges and lemons and figs and dates and olives and Smyrna raisins that lie about in great confusion. We need not remain hungry, however, for all these fruits are marvellously cheap. Think of buying as nice figs as you ever saw for four cents a pound, and choice seedless raisins for the same price.

We stop at the end of the street and gaze at the beautiful Parthenon, which rises against the clear blue of this Southern sky; and then, after passing two or three Greek churches, we enter our hotel.

## HOW PEOPLE TRAVEL IN GREECE.

People who live in Athens do not take the express train for Marathon, or a sleeping-car for Thermopylæ.

There is but one railroad in all Greece (1883), and that is only five miles long and was five years in building. It extends from the Piræus, which is the harbor of Athens, to the city, running part of the way on the line of the Long Walls that Themistocles built so many centuries ago.

This is a very short "through line," and does not run "lightning expresses;" but I dare say some of our American railroad kings would be glad to own it, for it pays twelve per cent dividends.

Wherever there is a road, one can go by carriage; and if he starts from Athens, he will have a good carriage and small but fairly good horses. If he starts from any other place, he may ride in some Noah's family carriage, and his horses may be dressed in old clothes-lines, instead of black leather harnesses with silver-plated buckles and rings.

Where there are no carriage-roads the usual way of travelling is on horses.

"We wanted to go from Athens," wrote Charlie Noble to Charlie Leland of his experience, "into the interior of the country. We went to a man who kept horses, and made a bargain with him for three horses and the services of a guide. His word was not a sufficient guarantee that he would keep his engagement; so, as has been the custom for centuries in the East, he gave us a certain amount of money, called *kaparo*, or earnest money, which we were to keep until we paid him at the end of the journey.

"The next morning, George, the guide, came with the horses.

"After leaving the good roads near Athens, we found only bridle-paths; and these, much of the way over the mountains, were rough and dangerous. The Greeks very appropriately call such a path *kake skala*, or 'bad stairs.'

"We occasionally met a peasant and his donkey, laden with small casks of wine or of olive oil for the market. At noon we were glad to sit under the shadow of a rock, and eat the lunch brought from Athens.

"At night we stopped at a small village. There was no hotel, not even a country tavern; but the Greeks are very hospitable, and several people gathered around, and invited us to their houses.

"Desiring to be in good company, we went home with the priest of the village. Greek priests, unlike Catholic priests, marry, and have families.

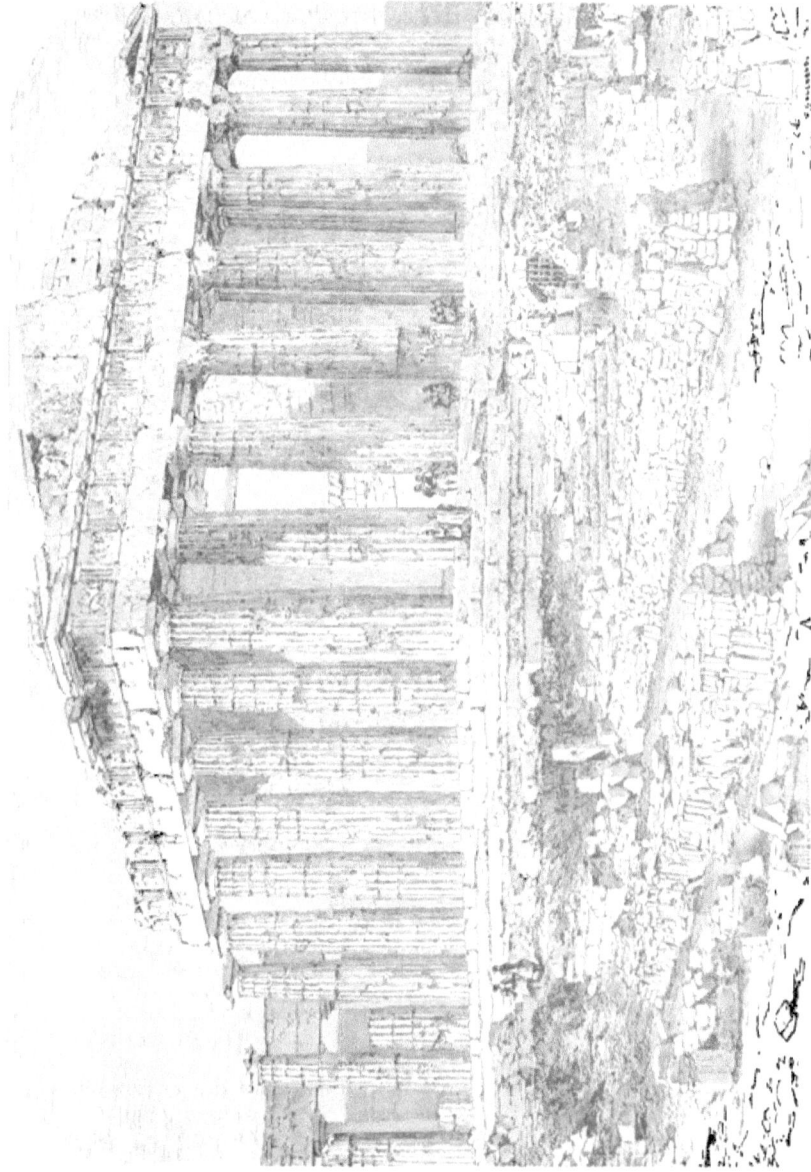

"They could offer us no supper; but George brought two live chickens, and killed and roasted them. We had bread and coffee in our bags, and the priest's wife gave us the use of a tin cup and the live coals on the hearth. Then we bought a little goat's milk, and altogether had a good supper.

"As we sat before the fire, George told the old priest, who was very ignorant, that we came from America, a country where it is noon when it is six o'clock at evening in Greece. 'How can this be?' said the priest. We tried with our closed hand to explain to him that the world was round, and turned on its axis every twenty-four hours, and also the relative positions of Greece and America, when, to our surprise and amusement, he exclaimed, as a child among us might have done, 'How, then, do people keep from falling off?

"When bedtime came, the 'strangers from America' were offered the spare-chamber of the house, and where do you think it was? The middle of the floor in the general sitting-room.

"The priest and his wife slept on one side of the room, we in the middle, and the children of the family on the other side. They furnished us mats for beds, and goat-skins to throw over us; and we rolled up our own blankets for pillows. To be sure, these were not 'downy beds of ease;' but a hard day's work had prepared us to forget our surroundings, and we were soon dreaming of soft mattresses and pleasant homes in America.

"As soon as we made our appearance in the street in the morning, we were surrounded by an eager group of men and boys, all having something to sell. The Greeks are always ready for a bargain. They knew we were going farther, and would want something for dinner. One man brought a live lamb, another some chickens, and another some goat's flesh, which the Greek peasants prefer to lamb, and often tried to sell us for lamb. We bought the lamb. George turned 'butcher and baker' again, and before long we were on the way, with our roasted lamb ready for the noonday meal.

"George told us we would find a good hotel at our next stopping-place; and although visions of carpets and spring beds did not flash before us, we hoped at least to be comfortable.

"On reaching the place it was dark, so that we were not able to judge of this grand hotel from its outward appearance. The room we first entered contained, to say the least, a great deal of furniture, but it was not like that usually seen in American hotels. On one side was a tub of soap and a barrel of salt-fish. On the shelves was the stock of a general store, from a ball of twine and a clay pipe to large water-jars, which the Greek women carry on their heads, and which look like those that Rebecca and her maidens carry in Biblical pictures.

"This room was indeed the great store of the place, where

HERMONTHIS.

everybody came to buy, and where everybody sat to talk over the news with the good-natured storekeeper and his pretty black-eyed wife.

"We were shown into the room out of this. It had no carpet on the floor and no windows. There were holes cut in the wall to let in the light and air, and these were closed at night with board shutters. There were three lounges, which were a luxury after sleeping on the floor.

"In the principal town where we stopped on this journey, the chief man, or mayor, to whom we had a letter of introduction, furnished us good beds and plenty to eat, and would take nothing for it.

"People who have plenty of time and like to walk often make journeys about Greece on foot.

"Would you know what we saw on this journey? We saw mountains, snow-capped and purple, in the distant atmosphere. We saw plains covered with growing cotton and groves of fig and olive trees and vineyards. We saw ruined fortresses and walls, built by the Greeks of ancient times; and we saw plenty of Greek boys and girls, who were very bright and curious to know all about us. Some of them could even speak a little English. One boy, seeing the nickel on my hand-bag, exclaimed, 'Plenty of money! plenty of money!' I doubt if there are many American boys who could speak as much modern Greek as that.

"Greece is a peninsula, with the beautiful blue sea almost all about it. The Ægean Sea on the east and the Adriatic on the west are dotted with numerous islands; and it is very pleasant, especially in the warm weather of summer, to go over to these islands, where one can get the sea-breeze continually.

"The Greek people have always loved the sea; and if you were to go into the harbor of Athens to-day, you would think they loved it still. There are innumerable boats of all kinds, from the small row-boat to the large steamer.

"It is a pretty sight to stand on the dock and see these boats, laden with oranges and other delicious fruits and sometimes having painted sails, float in and out on the blue water of the Ægean.

"Greek steamers are quite like any others, although not so large perhaps. If one wishes to take passage on a Greek steamer, he cannot go aboard from the dock, as the steamer is anchored out in the harbor, and he must be rowed to it in a small boat. If he wishes to leave the steamer at any island, he will find a crowd of small boats, with strange-looking boatmen in red fezes, waiting to carry passengers to shore. As the hackmen in New York ask if you want a 'kerridge,' so these boatmen all cry out, each one at the top of his voice, hoping to be heard above the others, and secure the greatest number of passengers.

"People of Greece prefer travelling by water, and so, instead of making excursions into the country, they take pleasure-trips to some of the islands.

"It will perhaps be many years before there are any more railroads in Greece; but we hope the time may come when, instead of trains of donkeys, the Greek people may see trains of cars, as we do in America.

"If Greece could only be connected with the railway system of central Europe, the number of tourists going to that classic land would be greatly increased. Perhaps that good time will not come until the Turk is driven 'bag and baggage' out of Europe."

AN ARAB BOY.

# CHAPTER XIV.

### THE NEW GREEK EMPIRE.

THE KING AND QUEEN OF GREECE. — THE NEW EMPIRE. A DAY AT MARATHON — OLD ALI BEDAIR'S STORY OF MARATHON.

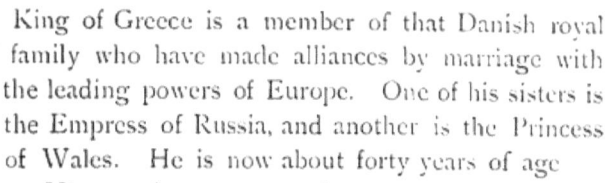

King of Greece is a member of that Danish royal family who have made alliances by marriage with the leading powers of Europe. One of his sisters is the Empress of Russia, and another is the Princess of Wales. He is now about forty years of age.

His youth was romantic, as was the youth of the several members of the Danish royal family. When the throne of Greece was left vacant in 1863, it was offered to several European princes, — among them, the Duke of Edinburgh: it was as often declined.

Prince George of Denmark was then seventeen years of age. He was a popular prince, of a popular family; and notwithstanding his youth, the Greeks, on the 6th of June, 1863, offered him the historic crown of their country, and the lad accepted it.

He found Greece full of factions; but he brought to the government the ardor and vigor of youth, with a maturity of judgment far beyond his years. His wisdom grew, and Greece to-day is one of the best-governed countries in Europe.

"Whom shall the handsome young king of Greece marry?" was asked in every court of Europe.

The success of his government was now assured, and over his little kingdom hung the romance of three thousand years. His hand was worthy of a noble princess. He did not let the courts choose for him. His heart made the choice. He had met, and had learned greatly to admire, a young Russian Princess, Olga, daughter of the Grand Duke Constantine, and niece of the Czar.

They had become friends; the friendship ripened into love. She accepted his hand; and the young king's choice seemed to please all the courts of Europe, and he was married to the handsome princess in 1867.

The new queen had good sense as well as beauty, and her delightful home-life commended her to the Greeks. The King and Queen of Hellenes have now five children, and their eldest son is the Duke of Sparta.

There are two reasons why Greece is, or should be, a country of peculiar interest to us. One is, that it is the land of the most noble and august ancient memories. Its heroes, its philosophers, its literature, and its great deeds of old make its renown dear even to our remote generation.

The second feature of its interest lies in the fact that after many centuries of abasement and torpor, Greece has, within the past sixty years, revived its energies and shown a new and rapid growth. It has become free; and it has established a constitutional government, under which its progress has been very marked.

When Greece, however, became independent of Turkish rule, a part of the territory inhabited by Greeks still remained, and remains to this day, under the Sultan's dominion. At the time of the Russo-Turkish war the Greeks were anxious to seize the opportunity to wrest this territory from the Turk. But the great powers prevailed on Greece to refrain from declaring war against Turkey, and held out the hope that when the Eastern troubles were settled, Greece would obtain at least a portion of the desired territory.

At the Congress of Berlin, which met to settle the terms of peace between Russia and Turkey, Greece put in its claim. It was warmly sustained by France and Italy; but none of the other powers would agree to compel Turkey to give up any territory to Greece. They did, however, all agree to recommend to the Sultan to satisfy his neighbor by some concession.

Time went on, and the Sultan delayed taking the advice of the Congress. Meanwhile Greece became restive and impatient; and a large proportion of the people clamored for war with Turkey, so as to acquire the territory by force.

Then a Conference of the powers met at Berlin, and proceeded to mark out a line on the map, and to urge upon Turkey to yield all the territory on the south of that line to Greece. This line passed nearly midway between the line up to which Greece claimed that her frontier should extend and that up to which the Sultan agreed that he would cede.

The Sultan refused to accept the advice of the Conference, as he had already done that of the more important body, the Congress. Ever since this refusal, negotiations, aided by the envoys of the other powers, have been going on between Turkey and Greece.

The national spirit of Greece has somewhat revived under the vigorous example of King George. The nation has striven again and again for independence from her Mohammedan oppressors. Her day of emancipation is gradually appearing, despite the dark omens of the past. As Epaminondas said to his timid generals, quoting from Homer, —

"His sword the brave man draws,
And knows no omen but his country's cause."

## A DAY AT MARATHON.

Marathon! Almost every school-boy is familiar with the story of *that* day, and has paid the tribute of his first efforts in oratory to Leonidas. So proud were our young tourists of their visit to the mound of the ancient heroes, that Charlie Leland wrote to Master Lewis and the pupils of the old school at Yule an account of it, and enclosed in the letter anemones from the plain.

ATHENS, April —.

DEAR TEACHER AND PUPILS OF YULE, — It is indeed a pleasure to me to be able to write to you from this city an account of a day at Marathon.

It was early, one bright morning in April, when four of us packed ourselves and our lunch-basket into a two-horse carriage, and started for a drive of twenty-two miles, from Athens to Marathon.

A FOUNTAIN IN GREECE.

April in Greece is like May in New England; and as we drove out of the city, the warm sun gave us a morning welcome, and the fresh breeze patted us on the cheek. The morning clouds, that lay like huge fleeces of white wool on the mountain-tops, were dyed rose-color and crimson and gold by the magic touch of the sun.

We rode through a narrow plain, with mountains on either side. On the right was Hymettus, where the wild bees have lived for thousands of years, and where they still make honey for the Athenians to eat.

RUINS OF A TEMPLE IN GREECE.

On the left was the mountain range of Pentelicus, containing the quarries that furnished beautiful marble for the buildings of old Athens, and from which the rich people of Athens still build their houses.

As we rode along into the more desolate part of the country, where trees and underbrush shut us in on either side, we opened our eyes wide, and peered into the bushes, half expecting to see a band of robbers, or brigands, ready to spring upon us.

The story was fresh in our minds, how, ten or more years ago, a company of English ladies and gentlemen started for Marathon, and somewhere near this part of the road, were seized by a band of brigands and hurried away to the mountains. The ladies and one man were allowed to return to Athens ; but the brigands refused to give up the other four men without a large sum of ransom money.

After a few days a company of Greek soldiers marched out to rescue the men ; and when the brigands discovered this, they killed the Englishmen, and threw the bodies into the bushes.

We asked our driver if he would show us where this happened.

He said, " Oh, yes, I was driving one of the carriages on that very day ; " and when we reached the spot, he stopped and pointed out where the brigands were concealed in the bushes, and the direction in which they hurried their captives away. We looked sharply into the bushes, and as far away as the eye could reach, but saw nothing that seemed like brigands, save a few men and women, in very peculiar costume, working the fields.

The Greek Government had to pay at that time so large a sum of money to the friends of the murdered men, that since then they have put an end to brigandage in Greece proper. The newspaper reports that we sometimes read of men being seized by brigands in Greece, can refer only to that part of the country which is still ruled by the Turks.

After a little, the carriage stopped for fresh horses. These had been sent on ahead ; and we found them, not in a stable or barn, — for there was none, — but tied to the branches of trees, awaiting our arrival.

The fresh horses started on with a livelier pace, and soon brought us where we could see for the remaining distance the plain of Marathon, walled on one side by an amphitheatre of mountains and washed on the other by a semicircular bay, whose waters are bluer and more beautiful than any we see in America.

As a background on the east, stretches the long island of Euboea, with its snow-capped mountain-peak, making of the whole a complete and beautiful picture.

We could not look at all this without thinking how, one afternoon in September, twenty-three hundred years ago, this little plain was the scene of one of the world's most important battles.

Here were landed one hundred and ten thousand Persian soldiers, who hoped to march to Athens, take possession of the city, and thus conquer the entire country.

But on the mountains, in the rear, were encamped ten thousand Greek soldiers, who rushed upon these Persians like hungry lions upon their prey, and drove them, a part into the marshy ground on either side of the plain, and a part back to their ships.

As the Persians sailed away, a glittering shield was seen to flash from one of the mountain-tops. Miltiades, the Greek general, thought this had been placed there by an enemy, as a signal to the Persians to sail to Athens and take the city, while the army was away. He therefore marched the Greeks, during the night, across the plain, a distance of twenty-two miles, and reached Athens just in time to see the Persian fleet enter the bay.

When the Persians saw, standing on the heights above, the very men who had defeated them at Marathon, they sailed away home, and left the little Greek army to take care of its own country.

In this battle the Greeks killed sixty-four hundred Persians, but the Persians only killed one hundred and ninety-two Greeks. These one hundred and ninety-two men were buried on the plain; and a high mound, which stands to this day, was raised over them.

As all these facts rushed through our minds, we threw back the carriage top. We stood up and tried to conclude on which one of the mountain-tops the bright shield appeared, and where on the plain the Greek army stood; but no one of the dead Greek warriors rose to tell us anything about it, and so we had to sit down unsatisfied, especially as we were in danger of losing our hats by the strong wind blowing from the plain.

If Marathon were in America, some enterprising Yankee would long ago have erected a great hotel, and lined the shore of the bay with pleasure-boats; but as it is in Greece, there is found only a stable for the horses, and man is supposed to know enough to care for himself.

We took our lunch-basket, and walked over a field of stubble and through a vineyard, to the mound.

This mound is thirty feet high, and six hundred feet in circumference at the base. One side of the top has been broken away, so that it is no longer perfect in form.

As we approached, it looked like one great flower-bed; for the bright anemones of every color covered its surface to the very top. We climbed nearly to the top, on the shady side, and, spreading our blankets on the ground, sat down for lunch.

We had scarcely opened our basket before there appeared, crouching on the ground near by, two curious little creatures, so oddly dressed that it was difficult to tell whether they were girls or boys. Their faces were so near the color of the ground that we concluded they must be relatives of Adam, for they certainly seemed made of the "dust of the earth."

As we threw our half-picked chicken bones and bits of oranges to them, their black eyes sparkled with joy, and their smiling lips revealed teeth so white and regular that any American boy or girl might have coveted a similar treasure.

Our little brown friends remained with us all the afternoon. They helped us pick and arrange the bright anemones; they gathered shells; they ran away to the plain and came back with their arms full of beautiful wild jonquils for which they expected some reward; and when we laid a Greek coin equal to five cents into their hands, they were utterly bewildered to see so much money all for themselves.

These were not the only children whose acquaintance we made at Marathon.

Off on the plain were feeding three or four hundred sheep, watched by shepherd boys and dogs. These boys, like all children, and especially like all Greek children, were curious to see who these strangers were, and, not daring to leave their sheep, drove them all up to the mound.

The sheep admired anemones as well as we; and we were glad that we had picked all we wanted, when we saw the beautiful bright blossoms nipped off.

These boys carried in their hand the shepherd's crook, which the old Greek poetry tells us about; and the sticks looked old enough to have been the very ones of which the poets sang. They also had on shoes that were large enough and old enough to have belonged to the shepherds of ages ago.

Their dress was a kind of brown coarse gown, something like a girl's dress, and their heads were bound up in yellow and red cotton handkerchiefs.

These boys remained in the field night and day; for you know there are no fences in that country, and it is necessary to watch the sheep all the time, to prevent them from straying away.

When the shepherd boy calls, the sheep know his voice and will follow him, but they do not know a stranger's voice. This is what Christ refers to in the tenth chapter of John, where he says, "My sheep hear my voice, and I know them, and they follow me.".

It is interesting to know that in Greece and the Eastern countries sheep are watched and tended and put into folds just as they were in the ancient time.

But there were other objects of interest to us in this visit to Marathon besides Greek shepherd boys and the contents of our lunch-basket.

We went to the shore and looked out on the clear blue water, and tried to imagine how it must have looked, covered with strange Persian war-ships. We picked up shells on the beach. We pressed our anemones to bring home to America. We walked around the mound, and were seized with a strong desire to dig into it and see if there were any bones or treasures of the old Greek warriors still remaining. We climbed to the top of the mound, and looked off on the beautiful picture, — than which, I believe, there is none fairer, — a picture of azure sky, snow-capped and purple-veiled mountains, blue water, and variegated plain, mottled with flocks of grazing sheep; and there came to us the lines of Lord Byron, —

> "The mountains looked on Marathon,
> And Marathon looked on the sea."

We thought we would like to be King George for a little while, just long enough to surround this mound with a fine marble railing from Mount Pentelicus, and place a monument on the top, from which should float the flag of the Greeks.

The Greek king and the Greek people have left the mound at Marathon uncared for; but Nature, in her sweet care for all things, has thrown over it a many-hued mantle of bright anemones.

There are living on the plain only shepherds, who till the fields and tend their sheep. These shepherds relate, with all sincerity, the old story that has always been believed, that at night warriors rise on the plain, and there is heard the clashing of steel and the neighing of horses; and so the battle is often fought over again.

Perhaps some one is asking, Why was the battle of Marathon one of the most important in the world's history?

When this question comes to you, stop and try to think what you know about the people who live in Asia at the present time, and then remember that the old Persians were Asiatics, and a semi-barbarous race. If the Persians had been victorious in the battle of Marathon, they might have overrun Europe, and the manners and customs of Europe would have been like those of Asia.

Had Greece become a Persian province, the Greeks could never have been the teachers of the world in politics, in literature, and in art. We must remember, also, that what Greece did for Europe, she did for us too; for we inherit European civilization.

The whole world should therefore rejoice that the ten thousand Greek soldiers sent the great Persian horde back to their Asiatic home, and left Europe to receive the impress of Greek culture.

## OLD ALI BEDAIR'S STORY OF MARATHON.

Thought has wings; it can go back to the past. Let us fly back over the events of thousands of years, to the Athens of the philosophers, poets, and heroes.

What is the scene? The city is white with temples. Over all rises a hill, with temples, — a mountain of marble so bright that it dazzles the eye.

There are palaces, gardens, statues everywhere.

The city is a camp now. There are armed men hurrying to and fro, and sentinels in bright armor. Anxiety is in every face.

It is not like a camp of to-day; it is even less savage, and more splendid and poetic.

Trumpets sound; the soldiers are putting on their armor; grooms are leading out restive horses; captains and generals are shouting their commands.

Everywhere are tents. Some of these are marked by ensigns; and in them men of noble stature are putting on their breastplates, helmets, and swords. The armor is of polished brass. The heroes come out and stand in the doors of their tents, glittering in the sun, and seeming, indeed, more like gods than men. A great shout goes up, —

"Miltiades!"

The soldiers are armed with spears. These are very heavy, and some twelve feet long.

The trumpets sound again. The chiefs take their shields of brass.

The common soldiers form; they have shields of leather, and are armed with spears.

It is a glorious morning; the mountain peaks glow in the sun. The people of the city are in the streets; there is agitation everywhere.

"To-day will begin another siege of Troy," said one of the old heroes. "The days of Hector and Priam have returned again."

"The sea is white with sails," said another. "So say the messengers. Such an army before never darkened the shores of Attica."

"He has landed,—the Great King," passed from lip to lip.

"Where?"

"At Marathon."

Trumpets, glittering chiefs, and a hurrying army. Solemn and grand is the march from Athens to Marathon. Wives, children, and relatives view, with tears, the departing army.

"They will never return again," passed from lip to lip. "What are they to the hosts of the King of Persia,—the king of all the earth?"

"Battles are won by valor, not numbers," said the sages. "They will come back again, and bring joy to the temples of the gods and heroes."

The gay plumes and glittering chiefs disappeared from view. The trumpets became only faint echoes from the hills. Prayers and offerings filled the temples of the gods.

"If we are defeated, Athens is lost," was repeated everywhere.

Women wailed in the streets.—

"O Athens, Athens, thy life is in the heroes; thy hope is in the strength of their spears. May the gods fight with the heroes to-day, O Athens, Athens!"

The little army of Greeks occupy the heights in sight of the sea. There on the calm blue waves floated the armaments of Persia, that had come to overwhelm Athens and the free States of Greece. Behind were the green hills and the marble city.

The Greek army is small. There is no grand array of cavalry, no sweeping curve of glittering chariots and charioteers. It is men who are to fight to-day. The period of spectacular armies has not yet come.

The Persian army is drawn up in battle array along the shore. It is vast and splendid, and behind it is the fleet. It is composed not only of Persians, but of warriors from the many nations over whom Persia bears sway. Its chiefs are confident of victory. The Persian king believes that Athens is already within his power.

The army is bright with champions in armor, with chariots and charioteers. The soldiers are armed with javelins. They have shields of immense surface, some of them so large as to cover the whole body.

The Persian army are spread out, and fill a great field. The Greeks are drawn into solid compact columns. The one army seems vastly larger than it is; the other much smaller.

The Persians have drawn up a large part of their fleet to the shore. They will need it there in case of retreat. Yet they do not dream of disaster. What can the little Greek army of infantry on the heights do against all this armament of champions, of cavalry, of chariots, and ships? The Persians are a hundred thousand strong; the Greeks but ten thousand.

There are solemn ceremonies in the Greek camp. The shout goes up: —
"Miltiades! Athens!"
The Greek orators address the soldiers.
"Miltiades!"
An altar smokes, and a sacrifice is performed.
"Athens!"
A song arises, — a song to the gods for the liberties of Greece. All is ready now for the army to descend upon the plain. The march begins; the soldiers cheering their hero, —
"Miltiades!"

Like the sweep of an eagle the Greek army rushes down upon the Persian host, shouting the names of gods and heroes. It is compact, resolute, desperate. A Greek to-day must be equal to ten Persians.

The Greeks run upon the scattered army of the Persians, uttering fierce cries. The Persians are thrown into a panic.

The Persians move backward towards the sea. The Greeks deal death and destruction everywhere. The Persians fly towards their ships. Six thousand are slain, while only about two hundred of the victorious Greeks fall.

Greece is victorious. Messengers fly back to Athens. Women and children rejoice. There are thanksgivings in the temples of the gods. Athens has withstood Asia. Greece is free.

Marathon is thenceforth to be the watchword of heroes.

> "The flying Mede, his shaftless broken bow;
> The fiery Greek, his red pursuing spear;
> Mountains above, earth's, ocean's, plain below;
> Death in the front, destruction in the rear."

"Can you see the scene as it was of old?"

"I can, I can," said several of the boys. Old Ali Bedair's description was enforced by his expression of face and his gestures, so that the class seemed not only to see the scene, but to hear the ancient shout, —

"Miltiades!"

From Athens, Charlie Noble and his companion went to Smyrna, and there connected with the steamer sailing for America direct, stopping only at the European Mediterranean ports, — a voyage of about three weeks. The course on the Atlantic was southerly; the weather mild, and the voyage a long pleasure. Rough weather and seas were experienced only on approaching New York. The boys had seen Alexandria, Cairo, the ruins of Memphis and Thebes, Jerusalem, Bethlehem, and Athens, and had entered nearly all the great seaports of the Mediterranean, — Genoa, Marseilles, and Gibraltar, — and at the last port had landed and visited the fortress. The time occupied was about three months. The journey was an education for a lifetime.

www.ingramcontent.com/pod-product-compliance
Lightning Source LLC
Chambersburg PA
CBHW022111230426
43672CB00008B/1349